BEYOND FINTECH

The Broader Impact of Technology on Society

Nurudeen D. Nurudeen

Copyright © 2024 All rights reserved. Nurudeen D. Nurudeen

Beyond Fintech: The Broader Impact of Technology on Society

No part of this book may be reproduced or transmitted in any form or by any means, electronic or mechanical, including photocopying, recording, or by any information storage and retrieval system, without permission in writing from the Copyright owner.

Any information is to be used for educational and information purposes only. It should never be substituted for financial advice.

The author or publisher does not in any way endorse any commercial products or services linked from other websites to this book.

Globally Available

Published by:
Emphaloz Publishing House
www.emphaloz.com
publish@emphaloz.com

ISBN: 978-3-5688-4682-2

A catalogue record of this book will be available from the National Library of Nigeria.

Reviews

"Nurudeen Nurudeen's 'Beyond Fintech' is an insightful and timely examination of technology's role beyond the financial sector, presenting a refreshing and much-needed narrative on the ethical and societal responsibilities that come with rapid digital advancement. Nurudeen's deep expertise shines through each page, making this book a must-read for anyone interested in understanding the broader implications of the technology that shapes our lives."

Dr. Amina Roberts, Professor of Digital Studies, University of Port Harcourt

"'Beyond Fintech' is a masterclass in articulating the impact of technology on various sectors in society. Nurudeen's understanding of complex systems and his ability to convey these ideas with clarity make this book an invaluable resource for professionals and laypeople alike. The book is both an eye-opener and a roadmap for embracing technology's potential while remaining vigilant to its societal impact."

James Ugu, CEO of InnovateX Solutions

"Nurudeen's book brilliantly tackles the transformation occurring in every facet of our lives due to technology. With thoughtful analysis and powerful insights, 'Beyond Fintech' dives into areas such as smart cities, education, and healthcare with an empathetic yet critical eye. This book is essential reading for anyone who wants to keep pace with technology's evolving role in society."

Sarah Zina, Technology Columnist, Tech News Daily

"'Beyond Fintech' stands out for its balanced approach to technology, presenting both the immense benefits and the ethical challenges that accompany modern advancements. Nurudeen's expertise and unique perspective offer a thoughtful narrative that encourages readers to reflect on the ethical responsibilities that accompany technological progress. This book is a critical addition to the conversation on how we should approach innovation."

Dr. Ethan Chinedu, Director of the Center for Technological Ethics

"With 'Beyond Fintech,' Nurudeen Nurudeen offers a thought-provoking exploration of technology's reach into every aspect of our lives. His perspective on the digital divide, societal responsibility, and the future of work makes this book particularly relevant in today's globalized world. It's an inspiring call to action for both individuals and organizations to pursue technology that serves the common good."

Emily Ogowu, Co-founder of Future Society Initiatives

PREFACE

In an era where technology permeates every facet of our lives, understanding its impact on society has never been more critical. The rapid pace of innovation has brought about significant changes not only in the way we conduct business but also in how we interact, learn, work, and live. These changes are profound and far-reaching, affecting not just individuals but entire industries and communities. While fintech has captured much attention as a transformative force within the financial sector, the influence of technology extends far beyond. It is not confined to the financial world but is deeply embedded in the very fabric of our society. This book, "Beyond Fintech: The Broader Impact of Technology on Society," is an exploration of this broader impact, aiming to shed light on how technology is reshaping various sectors and what this means for the future of our world, our societies, and our individual lives.

The motivation for this book stems from observing the profound changes occurring across multiple industries, driven by technological advancements. These changes are not isolated; they are interconnected and have ripple effects that extend far beyond their initial impact. While fintech serves as a prime example of how technology can disrupt traditional practices, it is merely the tip of the iceberg. The real story lies in the ripple effects of these innovations on society as a whole. Technology is not just changing how we do business; it is altering our social structures, our cultural norms, and even our understanding of what it means to be human in a rapidly evolving world. This book is a journey through the intersections of technology with healthcare, education, work, urban development, and more, offering insights into both the opportunities and challenges that lie ahead.

As we embark on this exploration, it is my hope that readers will gain a deeper understanding of the far-reaching implications of technology. This understanding is crucial not just for those working in technology-related fields but for everyone, as technology touches every aspect of our lives. The chapters that follow aim to provide a comprehensive overview of how technology is shaping our world, influencing not just industries but also societal norms, ethics, and global dynamics. This book serves as a call to action for individuals, businesses, and governments to harness technology responsibly, ensuring that its benefits are distributed equitably across society. The future we envision with technology must be one where progress is inclusive and where the benefits of innovation are shared by all, not just a select few.

Technology is a double-edged sword; while it offers incredible opportunities for growth and improvement, it also poses significant risks and challenges. As we move forward, it is essential to approach these challenges with a clear understanding of the potential consequences and with a commitment to using technology in ways that benefit humanity as a whole. The decisions we make today will shape the world of tomorrow, and it is up to us to ensure that the impact of technology is positive, sustainable, and inclusive.

Table of Contents

REVIEWS iii
PREFACE v
TABLE OF CONTENTS viii
FOREWORD x
INTRODUCTION xii

CHAPTER 1 1
The Evolution of Technology in Finance

CHAPTER 2 21
Digital Transformation in Healthcare

CHAPTER 3 37
Education in the Digital Age

CHAPTER 4 53
The Future of Work and Automation

CHAPTER 5 69
Smart Cities and Urban Development

CHAPTER 6 83
Technology's Role in Environmental Sustainability

CHAPTER 7 99
The Impact of Social-Media on Society

CHAPTER 8 113
The Ethical Implications of Artificial Intelligence

CHAPTER 9 ....**127**
The Rise of Blockchain and Decentralization

CHAPTER 10 ....**143**
The Global Digital Divide

ABOUT THE AUTHOR **157**

FOREWORD

In our era of unprecedented technological advancement, the impact of innovation is reshaping the world in ways that were once the realm of science fiction. Yet, amid the exhilaration of progress, there lies a pressing need to understand the profound societal shifts technology brings, not only within the realms of business and finance but across the very fabric of our daily lives. "Beyond Fintech: The Broader Impact of Technology on Society" by Nurudeen steps beyond the narrow lens of technological disruption in finance and offers readers a panoramic view of how these advancements influence sectors as diverse as healthcare, education, urban development, and environmental sustainability.

This book invites us to confront some of the most challenging questions about our digital age: How does technology redefine the parameters of human interaction? What are the ethical implications of deploying AI in sectors that influence human welfare, such as healthcare and criminal justice? How can we bridge the digital divide to ensure that technological progress benefits everyone, not just a select few? Nurudeen doesn't just touch on the surface of these questions; he dives deep, exploring each with a critical but compassionate eye, recognizing both the remarkable potential and the serious responsibilities that come with digital evolution.

Drawing from his extensive experience as a software engineer and an award-winning innovator, Nurudeen approaches these topics not merely as a theorist but as someone with an insider's view of the tech industry. He understands the transformative power of code and algorithms but never loses sight of the human consequences they entail. His insights are both sobering and empowering, as he argues for an approach to technology that is ethical, equitable, and inclusive. The thoughtful narratives and case studies throughout "Beyond Fintech" reveal that technology is not an impersonal force but a tool created and directed by human intention. Thus, he challenges readers whether policymakers, technologists, or everyday citizens to participate actively in shaping a future where innovation serves the collective good.

In an age where technological change often outpaces our ability to fully grasp its impact, this book provides a crucial roadmap for understanding and responsibly navigating the complex intersections of technology and society. For anyone looking to move beyond the buzzwords and explore the deeper implications of our digital age, "Beyond Fintech" is an essential and transformative read.

INTRODUCTION
The Intersection of Technology and Society

The dawn of the 21st century has been marked by a technological revolution that has transformed every aspect of human life. From the way we communicate to the way we work; technology has become an integral part of our daily existence. The reach of technology is vast and its influence profound, affecting every industry, every sector, and every corner of the globe. While much attention has been focused on fintech as a game-changer within the financial sector, the reality is that technology's impact is far more pervasive, influencing a wide array of sectors and fundamentally altering the fabric of society. This transformation is not just about the adoption of new tools or the creation of new industries; it is about a fundamental shift in the way we live, interact, and understand the world around us.

This book, "Beyond Fintech: The Broader Impact of Technology on Society," seeks to explore the many ways in which technology is reshaping our world. The changes we are witnessing are not just technological; they are social, cultural, and even philosophical. We will delve into the profound changes occurring in healthcare, education, the workplace, urban development, environmental sustainability, and more. Each of these sectors is undergoing a transformation that is driven by technology but that also has deep implications for society as a whole. The goal is to provide a holistic understanding of how technology is not only transforming industries but also redefining societal norms, ethics, and the way we interact with the world. This redefinition is ongoing, and its outcomes are still uncertain, making it all the more important for us to engage with these issues now.

As we explore these topics, it is essential to recognize that while technology offers immense opportunities for innovation and progress, it also presents significant challenges. These challenges are not just technical; they are ethical, social, and political. They range from ethical dilemmas and privacy concerns to the potential for job displacement and increased inequality. The purpose of this book is to examine both the positive and negative aspects of technological advancement, offering a balanced perspective on its broader impact on society. This balanced perspective is crucial because it allows us to celebrate the achievements of technology while also critically assessing its risks and drawbacks.

The chapters that follow will take you on a journey through the intersections of technology with various sectors, highlighting key innovations and their implications. From the evolution of technology in finance to the rise of smart cities, each chapter will provide insights into how technology is shaping the future. This journey is not just about understanding the past and present; it is about anticipating the future and preparing for the changes that are yet to come. By the end of this book, I hope you will have a deeper appreciation for the transformative power of technology and a clearer understanding of the responsibilities that come with it. This understanding is not just for technologists or policymakers; it is for everyone who is affected by technology, which is to say, all of us.

Technology is not neutral; it is shaped by the values and decisions of those who create and deploy it. As such, it is essential that we approach technology with a critical eye, asking not just what it can do, but what it should do. The future of technology is still being written, and we all have a role to play in shaping it. This book is an invitation to engage with the issues, to ask the hard questions, and to be part of the conversation about how we can harness the power of technology to create a better world for all.

CHAPTER 1
The Evolution of Technology in Finance

The financial sector has always been at the forefront of adopting and integrating new technologies. Historically, the evolution of finance has been closely tied to advancements in communication and information technology. From the earliest days of trade and commerce, where information was exchanged through messengers and written records, to the modern era of digital transactions and online banking, technology has been a driving force in shaping the way we manage, invest, and exchange value. This chapter traces the journey from the early days of manual banking to the digital age of fintech, highlighting the key innovations that have transformed the industry. This transformation has been both revolutionary and incremental, with each new technology building on the advancements of the past.

The story of technology in finance begins with the telegraph in the 19th century, a revolutionary tool that enabled the rapid transmission of financial information across great distances. The telegraph was not just a technological innovation; it was a game-changer for the financial industry, allowing for real-time communication between markets that were previously isolated by geography. This invention marked the beginning of a new era in finance, where information could be shared instantaneously, reducing the time lag between transactions and market reactions. The telegraph laid the groundwork for more sophisticated systems, such as the stock ticker, which provided real-time updates on stock prices and revolutionized stock trading. These early innovations set the stage for the development of a global financial system that is interconnected and highly responsive to changes in information.

The introduction of electronic funds transfer (EFT) in the mid-20th century further accelerated the pace of financial transactions. EFT systems allowed money to be transferred electronically between accounts, bypassing the need for physical cash or checks. This development not only improved the efficiency of financial transactions but also expanded access to banking services, particularly in remote or underserved areas. EFT was a precursor to the digital payment systems we use today, laying the foundation for a world where money can move at the speed of data. The impact of EFT on the financial industry cannot be overstated; it fundamentally changed the way people and businesses interact with money, making financial services more accessible and more efficient.

Automated teller machines (ATMs), introduced in the late 1960s, were another significant milestone in the evolution of financial technology. ATMs provided customers with 24/7 access to their bank accounts, allowing them to withdraw cash, check balances, and perform other basic banking functions without visiting a bank branch. This innovation not only enhanced customer convenience but also reduced the operational costs for banks, as fewer tellers were needed to handle routine transactions. ATMs were a critical step in the democratization of banking services, making it possible for people to access their money whenever and wherever they needed it. The success of ATMs paved the way for the development of other self-service banking technologies, such as online and mobile banking.

As the world moved into the digital age, the financial sector was quick to embrace the internet and mobile technology. The advent of online banking in the 1990s marked a turning point in how consumers interacted with financial institutions. For the first time, customers could manage their accounts, pay bills, and transfer money from the comfort of their homes. Online banking platforms offered unprecedented convenience, leading to widespread adoption and the gradual decline of traditional in-person banking. The shift to online banking was not just a technological change; it was a cultural shift, as people began to expect and demand digital access to their financial services.

Mobile banking, which emerged in the early 2000s, took this convenience a step further. With the proliferation of smartphones, consumers could now access their bank accounts on the go, making financial transactions more accessible and seamless. Mobile payment systems, such as Apple Pay and Google Wallet, further expanded the possibilities of mobile banking, allowing users to make purchases and transfer funds with a simple tap of their phones. The rise of mobile banking has had a profound impact on the financial industry, driving the development of new services and business models and challenging traditional banks to adapt to a rapidly changing landscape.

Peer-to-peer (P2P) lending platforms, such as LendingClub and Prosper, represented another significant innovation in the digital financial landscape. These platforms connected borrowers directly with lenders, bypassing traditional financial intermediaries like banks. P2P lending democratized access to credit, particularly for individuals and small businesses that might have been underserved by conventional financial institutions. By leveraging technology to match borrowers with lenders, these platforms reduced costs and offered more competitive interest rates. P2P lending is part of a broader trend towards the disintermediation of financial services, where technology enables people to access financial products and services directly, without the need for traditional middlemen.

The digital transformation of finance has brought about numerous benefits, including increased accessibility, convenience, and efficiency. However, it has also introduced new challenges and risks. One of the most significant challenges is cybersecurity. As financial transactions increasingly move online, the risk of cyberattacks and data breaches has grown. Financial institutions must invest heavily in security measures to protect their customers' sensitive information and maintain trust. The rise of digital finance has also raised important questions about privacy, data protection, and the role of regulators in ensuring that financial systems are secure and resilient.

Another challenge is the regulatory landscape. The rapid pace of technological innovation often outstrips the ability of regulators to keep up, leading to a complex and sometimes uncertain regulatory environment. Fintech companies, in particular, face the challenge of navigating a patchwork of regulations that vary by jurisdiction. As these companies continue to disrupt traditional financial services, there is an ongoing debate about the appropriate level of regulation to ensure consumer protection without stifling innovation. The balance between fostering innovation and ensuring stability is a delicate one, and how it is managed will have significant implications for the future of the financial industry.

Despite these challenges, the opportunities presented by technological advancements in finance are vast. Emerging trends such as blockchain, artificial intelligence, and decentralized finance (DeFi) are poised to further disrupt the financial sector. Blockchain technology, for example, has the potential to revolutionize everything from cross-border payments to supply chain management by providing a secure, transparent, and decentralized method of recording transactions. The implications of blockchain for the financial industry are still being explored, but it is clear that this technology has the potential to fundamentally change how we think about trust, security, and value exchange.

Artificial intelligence (AI) is another game-changer, with applications ranging from personalized financial advice to predictive analytics that can help institutions better understand and serve their customers. AI has the potential to transform the financial industry by automating complex tasks, improving decision-making, and creating new opportunities for innovation. However, it also raises important ethical questions about fairness, accountability, and the potential for bias in AI-driven systems.

DeFi, which leverages blockchain to create decentralized financial systems, offers the possibility of financial services that are more accessible, transparent, and resistant to censorship or corruption. DeFi is part of a broader movement towards decentralization, where technology is used to create systems that are not controlled by any single entity. The rise of DeFi has significant implications for the future of finance, as it challenges traditional financial institutions and creates new opportunities for innovation and inclusion.

The future of finance is likely to be shaped by these and other innovations, which will continue to challenge the traditional models of banking and finance. As we look ahead, it is clear that the intersection of technology and finance will remain a dynamic and evolving space, with profound implications for individuals, businesses, and society as a whole. The financial industry is at a crossroads, and the choices we make today will shape the future of finance for generations to come.

Through this exploration of the evolution of technology in finance, we gain a deeper understanding of how technological advancements have shaped the financial sector and how they will continue to influence its future trajectory. This understanding is crucial for anyone involved in finance, whether as a consumer, a professional, or a policymaker, as it provides the foundation for navigating the challenges and opportunities that lie ahead.

Blockchain: Beyond Cryptocurrency and Into Global Finance

Blockchain technology, originally devised as the backbone of Bitcoin, has rapidly evolved into a transformative force that goes well beyond cryptocurrencies. At its core, blockchain is a decentralized ledger system that allows multiple parties to hold a copy of the same data, maintaining transparency, security, and immutability. This innovation has reshaped the financial landscape by offering new ways to manage transactions, verify identities, and streamline processes, all while eliminating the need for intermediaries. Blockchain has brought an unprecedented level of transparency and security to finance, qualities that are now in demand for a range of applications far beyond digital currency.

One of blockchain's most significant impacts is in cross-border transactions. Traditionally, international money transfers require numerous intermediaries, including banks, clearinghouses, and foreign exchange providers, resulting in high fees and lengthy transaction times. Blockchain eliminates many of these intermediaries by providing a shared, immutable ledger that both parties can access in real time. For instance, Ripple, a blockchain-based payment protocol, enables instantaneous, low-cost cross-border payments that rival traditional systems like SWIFT. Through blockchain, individuals and businesses can transfer funds across borders in minutes rather than days, a development that has revolutionized international finance and opened new opportunities for global commerce.

In addition to speeding up transactions, blockchain technology is reshaping the concept of trust in financial systems. By decentralizing data storage and enabling consensus mechanisms, blockchain removes the need for traditional trust-based intermediaries, like banks, that have historically verified transactions. Instead, a blockchain-based system relies on cryptographic proofs and network consensus, making it nearly tamper-proof. For example, in traditional finance, asset verification—such as in real estate or stock ownership—can be time-consuming and prone to errors. Blockchain's transparent ledger allows for immediate verification of asset ownership, reducing fraud risks and making the process more efficient. This shift toward decentralized trust has inspired a wave of innovation in the financial sector, prompting banks and financial institutions worldwide to invest in blockchain research and development.

Another groundbreaking application of blockchain is in the creation of smart contracts. These self-executing contracts are programmed to automatically enforce agreements once specific conditions are met, eliminating the need for middlemen like lawyers or brokers. For instance, a smart contract on the Ethereum blockchain can automatically transfer property ownership to a buyer as soon as funds are received, streamlining transactions that traditionally involve manual verification. Smart contracts have broad implications for everything from real estate and supply chain management to insurance and legal settlements. By ensuring the automatic fulfillment of terms, smart contracts reduce human error, speed up processes, and lower costs, leading to increased efficiency across industries.

In recent years, the potential of blockchain has inspired central banks around the world to explore the idea of Central Bank Digital Currencies (CBDCs). Unlike cryptocurrencies like Bitcoin, CBDCs are state-backed and regulated digital currencies issued by central banks. For example, China's digital yuan, known as the Digital Currency Electronic Payment (DCEP), is a blockchain-inspired currency designed to facilitate cashless payments, increase transaction transparency, and improve the government's ability to monitor economic activity. Other countries, including Sweden and the Bahamas, have also launched their own CBDCs, marking a significant shift toward digital finance driven by blockchain principles. With CBDCs, governments are hoping to maintain the integrity and stability of their currencies while taking advantage of blockchain's transparency and efficiency.

Overall, blockchain technology is poised to redefine finance as we know it, offering solutions to issues like cross-border inefficiencies, transaction security, and transparency. Its ability to provide a decentralized, transparent, and secure system has implications that extend beyond finance, touching on fields as diverse as healthcare, supply chain management, and governance. As the world continues to explore and embrace blockchain's potential, the finance sector remains one of the most impacted, with every institution needing to consider how to integrate blockchain's capabilities into their operations. In many ways, blockchain is not just a technological innovation but a paradigm shift, changing the way value, trust, and assets are exchanged and stored.

Artificial Intelligence and Machine Learning: Personalized Banking in a Digital Age

Artificial intelligence (AI) and machine learning (ML) have introduced a new era of customization, efficiency, and security in financial services. These technologies enable banks and financial institutions to analyze vast amounts of data, extract meaningful insights, and make data-driven decisions that enhance customer experience. AI and ML have revolutionized various aspects of finance, from personalized customer service to fraud detection and credit scoring, bringing a level of precision and scalability that was previously unimaginable.

One of the most notable impacts of AI in finance is its ability to create highly personalized banking experiences. Using AI-driven algorithms, financial institutions can analyze customer behavior, spending patterns, and preferences to tailor services and products to each individual. For example, AI-powered chatbots provide 24/7 customer support, answering questions and resolving issues in real time. These chatbots learn from past interactions, enabling them to provide more accurate and efficient responses over time. By integrating these AI tools into their systems, banks can significantly reduce wait times for customers, providing support and assistance without the need for human intervention.

AI has also become an essential tool in credit scoring, enabling lenders to assess creditworthiness based on a wide range of variables, rather than relying on traditional scoring models alone. Traditional credit scores often fail to capture the full financial picture of an individual, particularly for those with limited credit history. AI-driven models can analyze alternative data, such as rent and utility payments, to provide a more comprehensive assessment of a borrower's ability to repay. This approach not only improves the accuracy of credit scoring but also expands access to credit for individuals who may have been previously overlooked. By incorporating real-time data and machine learning algorithms, AI-powered credit assessments can adjust dynamically, better serving underbanked populations and providing more inclusive financial services.

Fraud detection is another critical area where AI and ML are making substantial improvements. Financial fraud costs institutions billions of dollars annually, and traditional fraud detection methods often struggle to keep up with increasingly sophisticated tactics. AI-powered fraud detection systems use machine learning algorithms to analyze transaction patterns, flagging unusual behavior and stopping fraud in its tracks. Unlike rule-based systems, which can be bypassed with slight variations in tactics, machine learning algorithms can identify subtle, anomalous patterns that suggest fraudulent activity. Additionally, these algorithms improve over time, learning from new data and becoming more adept at identifying emerging fraud tactics. By employing AI in fraud detection, banks and financial institutions not only protect themselves but also provide a safer environment for their customers.

While the benefits of AI in finance are numerous, it also introduces new ethical challenges. One of the primary concerns is the potential for bias in AI-driven decisions. AI algorithms are only as unbiased as the data used to train them; if the data reflects societal biases, the algorithms can perpetuate these biases in credit approvals, loan terms, and customer service. Addressing this issue requires a proactive approach, including regular audits of AI systems, the use of diverse training datasets, and transparency about how algorithms make decisions. As AI becomes more embedded in finance, it will be crucial for financial institutions to prioritize ethical AI practices to ensure fair treatment for all customers.

The rise of AI in finance signals a shift toward a more intelligent, responsive, and personalized banking experience. From helping banks understand customer needs to enhancing security measures, AI and ML are reshaping the financial sector in profound ways. Financial institutions that harness these technologies are better equipped to meet customer expectations, improve operational efficiency, and stay competitive in an increasingly digital landscape. However, the responsibility to use AI ethically and transparently remains a central concern, underscoring the need for a balanced approach to innovation.

Decentralized Finance (DeFi): A New Frontier of Financial Services

Decentralized Finance, commonly known as DeFi, represents a groundbreaking approach to financial services that relies on blockchain technology to operate without traditional intermediaries like banks or financial institutions. By leveraging smart contracts and decentralized applications (dApps), DeFi platforms enable peer-to-peer financial transactions directly between individuals. This model offers a democratized and accessible financial ecosystem that provides services such as lending, borrowing, trading, and investing, all accessible to anyone with a smartphone and internet connection.

DeFi's impact is particularly significant in regions with limited access to traditional financial services. In many developing countries, millions of individuals are unbanked or underbanked, often because of a lack of physical infrastructure or restrictive requirements for opening a bank account. DeFi addresses these barriers by providing financial access through decentralized networks, allowing individuals to participate in financial activities directly from their mobile devices. For example, someone in a rural area without access to a bank can use a DeFi lending platform to obtain a loan, or they can invest in digital assets without needing a financial intermediary. DeFi opens doors for financial inclusion, empowering individuals to manage their wealth, access credit, and participate in the global economy.

Transparency is another core feature of DeFi, as all transactions are recorded on a public blockchain. Unlike traditional banking, where transactions are typically opaque, DeFi transactions are fully transparent and verifiable, fostering a higher level of trust among users. This transparency not only reduces the risk of fraud but also enables users to make informed decisions, as they can see how funds are managed and tracked on the blockchain. However, this transparency also raises privacy concerns, as transaction details, though pseudonymous, are visible on the public ledger.

Despite its transformative potential, DeFi faces significant challenges, including regulatory uncertainty and security vulnerabilities. Because DeFi operates outside the bounds of traditional finance, it often exists in a legal gray area, with varying regulations across jurisdictions. Additionally, DeFi platforms are vulnerable to security risks, as smart contracts—while autonomous can be susceptible to coding errors or malicious attacks. Cases of DeFi platform breaches have led to substantial financial losses, highlighting the need for rigorous security audits and robust coding practices. As regulators and developers work to address these issues, the DeFi ecosystem continues to grow, reshaping the financial landscape and challenging the role of traditional institutions.

DeFi is more than just a trend; it represents a fundamental shift toward decentralization, transparency, and inclusivity in finance. By enabling people to control their finances independently, DeFi has the potential to empower individuals, disrupt traditional financial systems, and create a more inclusive global economy. However, as DeFi continues to evolve, finding the balance between innovation and regulation will be essential to ensure the sector's sustainable growth.

Cybersecurity in Fintech: Defending Against the Digital Age's Growing Threats

The rise of digital finance has brought with it an urgent need for robust cybersecurity measures. As financial institutions shift toward online and mobile banking, they have become prime targets for cyberattacks, ranging from data breaches and identity theft to phishing scams and ransomware. Cybersecurity in fintech requires a multi-layered approach, encompassing both technology and policies, to protect sensitive customer information and ensure the integrity of financial transactions.

With the expansion of online banking, financial institutions are implementing increasingly sophisticated cybersecurity measures. Multi-factor authentication (MFA), for instance, has become a standard practice, requiring users to verify their identities through additional steps, such as biometric scans or one-time codes. By incorporating multiple layers of security, MFA significantly reduces the risk of unauthorized access. Encryption is another critical tool, protecting sensitive data by converting it into a coded format that only authorized parties can decipher. These security protocols are essential for defending against unauthorized access and maintaining customer trust in an era where personal information is highly vulnerable.

Artificial intelligence is also becoming an invaluable asset in cybersecurity. AI-driven systems can monitor transactions in real-time, detecting anomalies that may indicate fraudulent activity. For instance, if an account suddenly registers transactions from an unfamiliar location or makes unusually large withdrawals, an AI system can flag this behavior for further investigation. Machine learning algorithms continually improve by analyzing data, allowing these systems to detect new patterns of fraudulent behavior as they emerge. This proactive approach to fraud prevention enables financial institutions to respond quickly to potential threats and minimize the impact of cyberattacks.

However, the evolving nature of cyber threats requires constant vigilance. Hackers are continually developing new tactics to bypass security measures, making it essential for financial institutions to stay ahead by investing in the latest cybersecurity technologies. In response to these challenges, fintech companies are now prioritizing cybersecurity in their business models, recognizing that a single data breach can have severe financial and reputational consequences. The future of finance will depend on the sector's ability to adapt to new threats, underscoring the importance of cybersecurity as a pillar of digital finance.

The intersection of technology and finance has made cybersecurity indispensable. As the fintech landscape continues to expand, robust security measures are essential not only to protect consumer data but to uphold trust in the digital financial ecosystem. Cybersecurity in finance is more than just a protective measure; it is foundational to the integrity and resilience of the entire industry.

NURUDEEN D. NURUDEEN

CHAPTER 2
Digital Transformation in Healthcare

The healthcare industry is one of the most critical sectors where technology has made significant strides. The integration of digital tools and platforms into healthcare has not only transformed the way medical services are delivered but has also greatly improved patient outcomes. The impact of technology on healthcare is profound and multifaceted, affecting everything from the diagnosis and treatment of diseases to the management of healthcare systems and the delivery of care. In this chapter, we explore the profound impact of technology on healthcare, highlighting the key innovations that are reshaping the industry. These innovations are not just changing how we treat patients; they are redefining what is possible in medicine and challenging us to think differently about health and wellness.

One of the earliest and most impactful technological advancements in healthcare is the electronic health record (EHR). EHRs have revolutionized the way patient information is stored, accessed, and shared among healthcare providers. Before the advent of EHRs, patient records were often fragmented and difficult to access, leading to inefficiencies and errors in medical care. With EHRs, healthcare providers can access a patient's complete medical history at the click of a button, enabling more accurate diagnoses and personalized treatment plans. EHRs also facilitate better coordination of care, as multiple providers can access and update a patient's record, ensuring that everyone involved in the patient's care is on the same page.

Telemedicine is another technological innovation that has significantly transformed healthcare. Telemedicine allows healthcare providers to consult with patients remotely, using video conferencing and other digital communication tools. This technology has been particularly beneficial in rural and underserved areas, where access to healthcare services is often limited. Telemedicine has not only expanded access to care but has also reduced costs and improved patient satisfaction by making healthcare more convenient and accessible. The COVID-19 pandemic has accelerated the adoption of telemedicine, highlighting its potential to transform healthcare delivery and improve access to care.

Artificial intelligence (AI) and machine learning (ML) are also playing an increasingly important role in healthcare. AI-powered tools can analyze vast amounts of medical data to identify patterns and make predictions that can aid in diagnosis and treatment. For example, AI algorithms are being used to detect early signs of diseases such as cancer, often with greater accuracy than human doctors. In addition, AI is being used to develop personalized treatment plans based on a patient's genetic makeup, lifestyle, and other factors. The potential of AI in healthcare is vast, and we are only beginning to scratch the surface of what is possible.

Wearable technology is another area where digital transformation is having a significant impact on healthcare. Devices such as smartwatches and fitness trackers can monitor a person's vital signs, activity levels, and other health metrics in real-time. This data can be used to detect potential health issues early on and to provide patients with personalized recommendations for improving their health. Wearable technology is also being used to monitor chronic conditions, such as diabetes and heart disease, enabling patients to manage their health more effectively. The data collected by wearables can also be shared with healthcare providers, enabling more proactive and personalized care.

The integration of technology into healthcare has also led to the development of new treatment modalities. For example, 3D printing technology is being used to create customized prosthetics, implants, and even organs. Virtual reality (VR) is being used to treat conditions such as PTSD and chronic pain by immersing patients in therapeutic virtual environments. These and other innovations are expanding the possibilities of what is possible in medicine, offering new hope to patients with previously untreatable conditions. The potential of these technologies to improve patient outcomes and enhance the quality of life is enormous, and we are likely to see continued innovation in this area in the coming years.

However, the digital transformation of healthcare is not without its challenges. One of the biggest concerns is the issue of data privacy and security. As more patient information is digitized and shared across platforms, the risk of data breaches and cyberattacks increases. Healthcare providers must invest in robust cybersecurity measures to protect patient data and maintain trust. The consequences of a data breach in healthcare can be severe, not just in terms of financial loss but also in terms of patient safety and trust in the healthcare system.

Another challenge is the digital divide. While technology has the potential to greatly improve healthcare, not all patients have equal access to digital tools and services. For example, older adults and low-income individuals may lack the necessary devices or internet access to benefit from telemedicine and other digital health services. Healthcare providers must find ways to bridge this divide and ensure that all patients can benefit from technological advancements. This may involve developing alternative methods of delivering care or providing support to help patients access digital health tools.

Despite these challenges, the digital transformation of healthcare holds great promise. As technology continues to evolve, we can expect to see even more innovative solutions that improve patient outcomes, reduce costs, and make healthcare more accessible to all. The key will be to ensure that these advancements are implemented in a way that addresses the challenges and maximizes the benefits for all stakeholders. This will require collaboration between healthcare providers, technology companies, policymakers, and patients, as well as a commitment to using technology in ways that prioritize patient well-being and equity.

The potential of technology to transform healthcare is enormous, but realizing this potential will require careful planning, investment, and a focus on ethical considerations. As we move forward, it is essential to ensure that the benefits of digital health are shared by all, and that technology is used to enhance, rather than replace, the human elements of care. The future of healthcare is bright, but it is up to us to ensure that it is also equitable, sustainable, and centered on the needs of patients.

Telehealth and Remote Care: Reaching Patients Across Distances

Telemedicine, also known as telehealth, has transformed the landscape of healthcare by enabling patients to receive medical care without being physically present in a clinic or hospital. Through digital platforms such as video calls, secure messaging systems, and mobile applications, doctors and patients can now communicate effectively and diagnose, monitor, and treat a range of conditions remotely. This model has become particularly vital for patients in rural or underserved areas, where access to medical facilities is limited and travel to urban centers can be both time-consuming and costly. With telehealth, these patients can connect to specialists from any location, allowing for faster diagnosis and timely intervention that might otherwise have been unavailable.

The reach of telehealth extends well beyond individual consultations. Remote monitoring devices are being deployed to continuously track a patient's health metrics, from blood pressure and blood glucose levels to heart rate and oxygen saturation. Patients with chronic illnesses such as diabetes, heart disease, and respiratory conditions can now use wearable or at-home devices that send real-time data directly to healthcare providers. This constant flow of information enables physicians to track trends and identify changes in a patient's condition, allowing for proactive adjustments to treatment plans. Studies have shown that remote monitoring can significantly improve outcomes for patients with chronic conditions by preventing complications and hospital readmissions. Furthermore, remote monitoring provides a level of independence for patients, empowering them to manage their health effectively from home while staying connected to their healthcare team.

Mental health services have also seen significant growth through telehealth. Virtual therapy, counseling, and psychiatric consultations offer patients access to mental health professionals from the privacy and comfort of their homes, which can be especially helpful for those who may face stigma, lack of resources, or logistical barriers. Mobile applications focused on mental wellness provide 24/7 access to tools such as guided meditation, cognitive behavioral therapy exercises, and mood tracking, offering immediate support for those struggling with anxiety, depression, or stress. During the COVID-19 pandemic, the demand for virtual mental health services surged as individuals faced unprecedented levels of isolation and stress, highlighting telehealth's role in addressing mental health crises.

Despite its benefits, telehealth faces certain limitations. Effective telehealth services require reliable internet connectivity and access to technology, both of which can be barriers for low-income, elderly, or rural populations. Additionally, while telehealth is effective for general consultations and follow-ups, some medical assessments require physical interaction, such as palpation, imaging, or surgical intervention, which cannot be replicated virtually. There are also concerns about maintaining data privacy in telemedicine, as patient information is transmitted across digital platforms that must meet stringent security standards.

As telehealth continues to evolve, healthcare systems are exploring hybrid models of care that combine virtual and in-person visits to optimize patient outcomes. Governments and insurers are beginning to recognize the value of telehealth, with many expanding coverage and reimbursement policies to include virtual care. This shift underscores telehealth's growing role in healthcare, as it not only expands access but also fosters a more flexible, responsive, and patient-centered healthcare model that can adapt to the unique needs of each individual.

Artificial Intelligence in Diagnostics and Predictive Analytics

Artificial intelligence (AI) has introduced revolutionary advancements in healthcare, particularly in diagnostics and predictive analytics. AI-powered tools leverage machine learning algorithms to analyze complex datasets such as medical images, electronic health records, and genomic information to identify patterns that can aid in diagnosing diseases and predicting patient outcomes with a level of precision previously unattainable. In radiology, for instance, AI algorithms are being used to detect abnormalities in X-rays, MRIs, and CT scans. These algorithms can highlight areas of concern for radiologists, speeding up diagnosis for conditions such as fractures, tumors, or vascular blockages. Notably, AI is being deployed in the early detection of diseases like breast cancer, where it has shown the potential to catch subtle changes in mammogram that may be missed by the human eye.

Predictive analytics, another core application of AI, enables healthcare providers to anticipate patient needs and make proactive decisions. Through the analysis of patient demographics, lifestyle data, medical history, and genetic information, machine learning algorithms can forecast disease risk and suggest preventive measures. For instance, predictive models are being used to identify patients at high risk for chronic conditions such as diabetes, cardiovascular disease, and hypertension. This early identification allows for targeted interventions, reducing the likelihood of disease progression and improving long-term outcomes. In the context of hospital administration, predictive analytics is also optimizing workflows by forecasting patient admissions, scheduling staff effectively, and ensuring resources are allocated efficiently, which has led to significant cost savings and improved patient care.

AI is also pioneering personalized medicine, a field that tailor treatment plans based on the unique characteristics of each patient. Personalized medicine combines AI with genomic sequencing and clinical data to develop treatment strategies that are customized for each individual. In cancer care, for example, AI algorithms analyze genetic markers, tumor characteristics, and patient responses to previous treatments, allowing oncologists to identify the most effective therapies for each patient. This approach not only increases treatment efficacy but also minimizes adverse side effects by targeting therapies that are most compatible with a patient's genetic makeup and disease profile. Personalized medicine represents a shift toward more precise and effective care, with AI providing the computational power needed to analyze the vast amounts of data required to make these customized recommendations.

Despite its immense potential, AI in healthcare presents ethical and practical challenges. Ensuring the accuracy and fairness of AI-driven decisions is critical, as biased algorithms or flawed data can lead to misdiagnoses or unequal access to care. Data privacy is another significant concern, given the sensitive nature of medical information. Regulations and guidelines are essential to ensure that AI is used responsibly, balancing innovation with patient rights and ethical considerations. Nonetheless, the use of AI in diagnostics, predictive analytics, and personalized medicine is reshaping healthcare, providing tools that enhance accuracy, reduce costs, and ultimately improve patient outcomes on an unprecedented scale.

3D Printing and Customized Medical Solutions

3D printing, also known as additive manufacturing, is transforming healthcare by enabling the creation of customized medical solutions that can be tailored to the unique needs of each patient. Unlike traditional manufacturing, where products are created by cutting or molding materials, 3D printing builds objects layer by layer, allowing for intricate designs that can accommodate specific medical requirements. This technology has proven invaluable in creating personalized prosthetics, implants, and anatomical models, and is even advancing toward the fabrication of human tissues and organs, opening new possibilities in regenerative medicine.

Customized prosthetics and implants are among the most widespread applications of 3D printing in healthcare. For patients requiring artificial limbs or joint replacements, 3D printing allows for the production of prosthetics that are perfectly fitted to the patient's body. These prosthetics can be designed with the individual's specific anatomy in mind, improving comfort, mobility, and functionality compared to conventional, mass-produced options. For example, a patient requiring a hip replacement can receive a 3D-printed implant that matches the exact contours of their hip joint, reducing the risk of complications and enhancing the longevity of the implant. Similarly, dental implants and orthodontic devices, such as aligners, are increasingly being customized through 3D printing to fit each patient precisely, resulting in better outcomes and reduced treatment times.

Beyond prosthetics, 3D printing is revolutionizing surgical planning and education by enabling the production of detailed anatomical models based on a patient's medical scans. Surgeons can use these models to plan complex procedures, practice on replicas of the patient's anatomy, and anticipate potential challenges before entering the operating room. These models are especially valuable in cases involving intricate surgeries, such as those in neurosurgery, cardiology, or orthopedic reconstruction. By allowing surgeons to visualize and interact with a 3D model of the specific organ or structure they will be operating on, 3D printing enhances precision and reduces the risk of complications during surgery.

One of the most promising frontiers in 3D printing is bioprinting, a technique that uses bio-ink made from living cells to create tissue structures. While still in the early stages of development, bioprinting has the potential to address the critical shortage of organ donors by producing lab-grown tissues and, eventually, functional organs. Researchers are already exploring the use of bioprinting to produce skin grafts, blood vessels, and cartilage, which could be used to treat patients with severe injuries or degenerative diseases. The long-term goal is to produce fully functional organs, such as kidneys or livers, that could be transplanted into patients, offering a solution to the lengthy wait times and rejection risks associated with traditional organ transplants.

However, the adoption of 3D printing in healthcare is not without challenges. The technology is expensive, requiring significant investment in specialized equipment and materials. Additionally, the regulatory environment for 3D-printed medical devices is still evolving, with questions around quality control, safety, and standardization. Ethical considerations also arise with bioprinting, particularly regarding the creation of human tissues and organs. Despite these hurdles, 3D printing has demonstrated its potential to revolutionize healthcare by providing tailored solutions, improving surgical outcomes, and pushing the boundaries of medical science.

Data Privacy and Security in Digital Health

As healthcare becomes increasingly digital, the importance of data privacy and security has grown exponentially. Electronic health records (EHRs), telemedicine platforms, wearable devices, and mobile health apps all generate vast amounts of sensitive patient data, from medical histories and genetic information to real-time health metrics. This wealth of data offers tremendous potential for improving healthcare delivery, but it also introduces significant risks, as breaches in data security can lead to severe financial, legal, and reputational consequences. For patients, the compromise of personal health information can result in discrimination, financial fraud, and a loss of trust in healthcare providers.

The digitization of health records has improved efficiency, but it has also made healthcare systems more vulnerable to cyberattacks. Hackers often target healthcare organizations due to the high value of medical data, which can be exploited for identity theft, insurance fraud, or sold on the dark web. To counteract these threats, healthcare providers must implement robust cybersecurity measures, including encryption, firewalls, and intrusion detection systems. Additionally, multi-factor authentication (MFA) and data anonymization are increasingly being used to protect patient information, making it harder for unauthorized users to access or identify sensitive data. However, maintaining security in a complex healthcare environment with interconnected devices and networks remains a considerable challenge.

Regulatory frameworks such as the Health Insurance Portability and Accountability Act (HIPAA) in the United States and the General Data Protection Regulation (GDPR) in Europe mandate stringent standards for the protection of personal health data. These regulations impose heavy fines for non-compliance and require healthcare organizations to implement policies that protect patient privacy. For example, HIPAA mandates that healthcare providers restrict access to patient information, maintain data integrity, and report data breaches. However, compliance with these regulations is not always straightforward, especially for smaller healthcare providers that may lack the resources to invest in state-of-the-art cybersecurity measures.

Wearable devices and mobile health apps add another layer of complexity to data privacy concerns. These devices continuously collect personal health data, often sharing it with third-party apps or cloud storage services. While this data can provide valuable insights into an individual's health, its collection and storage by private companies raise questions about consent, data ownership, and potential misuse. Patients may not always be fully aware of who has access to their data or how it is being used, creating a need for greater transparency and informed consent processes. Ensuring that patients retain control over their data, while also protecting it from unauthorized access, remains a central challenge for digital health providers.

The future of healthcare will likely involve even more data-driven technologies, making data privacy and security essential pillars of digital health. As healthcare organizations continue to adopt new technologies, it is imperative that they establish comprehensive data protection strategies, invest in cybersecurity training, and prioritize transparency with patients regarding data usage. Only by addressing these security challenges can healthcare providers maintain public trust and fully realize the potential of digital health.

NURUDEEN D. NURUDEEN

CHAPTER 3
Education in the Digital Age

Education has always been a cornerstone of societal development, and with the advent of digital technology, the landscape of education is undergoing a profound transformation. The integration of digital tools into the educational process has the potential to democratize access to knowledge, enhance learning experiences, and prepare students for the challenges of the 21st century. In this chapter, we delve into the impact of technology on education, exploring the innovations that are reshaping how we learn and teach. These innovations are not just changing the way we deliver education; they are challenging us to rethink what education is, what it can be, and how it should be delivered in a rapidly changing world.

One of the most significant developments in education is the rise of e-learning platforms. These platforms, such as Coursera, Udemy, and Khan Academy, offer a wide range of courses that can be accessed online, often at little or no cost. E-learning platforms have democratized access to education, allowing people from all over the world to learn new skills and advance their careers. They have also provided an alternative to traditional classroom-based education, offering flexibility and convenience for learners with busy schedules or other commitments. The rise of e-learning is part of a broader trend towards lifelong learning, where individuals continually update their skills and knowledge to keep pace with a rapidly changing world.

Digital technology has also transformed the traditional classroom. Interactive whiteboards, tablets, and other digital tools are now commonplace in schools, enabling teachers to create more engaging and interactive lessons. These tools allow for a more personalized learning experience, as teachers can tailor their lessons to the needs and abilities of individual students. For example, students who struggle with certain subjects can receive additional support through online tutorials and exercises, while more advanced students can explore topics in greater depth. The use of technology in the classroom also allows for more collaborative and project-based learning, where students work together on real-world problems and develop critical thinking and problem-solving skills.

The rise of digital technology has also led to the development of new teaching methodologies. For example, the flipped classroom model, where students learn new content online at home and then apply that knowledge in the classroom through collaborative activities, has gained popularity in recent years. This model allows students to learn at their own pace and provides more opportunities for active learning and collaboration in the classroom. The flipped classroom is just one example of how technology is enabling new approaches to teaching and learning that are more flexible, personalized, and student-centered.

Another significant impact of technology on education is the rise of massive open online courses (MOOCs). MOOCs offer courses from top universities and institutions to a global audience, often for free or at a low cost. These courses have the potential to reach millions of learners who may not have access to traditional higher education. MOOCs have also opened up new opportunities for lifelong learning, allowing individuals to continue their education and stay up-to-date with the latest developments in their field. The rise of MOOCs is part of a broader trend towards the globalization of education, where knowledge and expertise are shared across borders and where learners can access the best educational resources from anywhere in the world.

Artificial intelligence (AI) is also making its mark on education. AI-powered tools can provide personalized learning experiences, adaptively assessing a student's progress and adjusting the content and pace accordingly. AI is also being used to automate administrative tasks, such as grading and scheduling, freeing up time for teachers to focus on instruction. Additionally, AI-powered tutoring systems can provide students with instant feedback and support, helping them to overcome challenges and achieve their learning goals. The potential of AI in education is vast, and we are likely to see continued innovation in this area in the coming years.

However, the digital transformation of education also presents challenges. One of the most pressing issues is the digital divide. Not all students have access to the devices and internet connectivity needed to participate in digital learning. This disparity can exacerbate existing inequalities in education, leaving some students behind. Addressing the digital divide is crucial to ensuring that all students have the opportunity to benefit from the advancements in educational technology. This may involve providing devices and internet access to students who need them, as well as developing offline and low-tech solutions for those in areas with limited connectivity.

Another challenge is the need for educators to adapt to new technologies and teaching methodologies. Integrating digital tools into the classroom requires teachers to develop new skills and approaches to instruction. Professional development and ongoing training are essential to help educators keep pace with the rapidly changing educational landscape. This may involve learning how to use new technologies, developing new pedagogical strategies, and staying up-to-date with the latest research on effective teaching and learning.

Despite these challenges, the potential benefits of digital technology in education are immense. By leveraging technology, we can create more inclusive, engaging, and effective learning environments that prepare students for the challenges of the future. As technology continues to evolve, it will be essential to ensure that these advancements are implemented in a way that maximizes their benefits while addressing the challenges and ensuring equitable access for all students. The future of education is bright, but it is up to us to ensure that it is also inclusive, equitable, and centered on the needs of learners.

The role of education in society is more important than ever, and the integration of technology into education is a critical part of ensuring that all individuals have the opportunity to succeed in a rapidly changing world. As we move forward, it is essential to keep the focus on the needs of learners and to use technology in ways that enhance, rather than replace, the human elements of education. The future of education is not just about technology; it is about people, and about ensuring that everyone has the opportunity to learn, grow, and thrive in a rapidly changing world.

E-Learning Platforms: Breaking Down Barriers to Education

E-learning platforms have fundamentally changed the way individuals around the world access education, creating pathways for students and professionals alike to acquire knowledge, develop skills, and earn certifications, regardless of geographic or economic barriers. Platforms such as Coursera, Udemy, and Khan Academy have democratized education by offering courses in a range of subjects from data science and digital marketing to philosophy and the arts—often at minimal or no cost. In developing regions, where access to quality education and expert instructors is often limited, these platforms allow students to access courses from world-renowned universities and industry leaders, gaining valuable skills that were previously inaccessible.

Flexibility is a hallmark of e-learning, as these platforms allow learners to study at their own pace, making education more accommodating to the needs of diverse learners. This flexibility is particularly valuable for non-traditional students, such as working professionals, parents, or individuals with disabilities, who can now pursue their educational goals without the constraints of traditional, rigid class schedules. Furthermore, the interactive nature of many e-learning courses, including video lectures, discussion forums, interactive quizzes, and hands-on projects, fosters engagement and allows learners to actively participate in their own education. Many platforms also provide progress tracking and certificates upon completion, which can add significant value to a learner's resume, helping them advance in their careers or transition into new fields.

The emergence of e-learning has also contributed to the rise of lifelong learning, a trend that emphasizes continuous skills development throughout one's career. As the global economy rapidly evolves and new technologies emerge, the skills required by employers are constantly changing. E-learning allows professionals to stay updated with the latest industry developments, gaining specialized knowledge in fields like artificial intelligence, blockchain, and cybersecurity, thereby maintaining their relevance and competitiveness in the job market. Some companies have even started partnering with e-learning providers to offer tailored training programs, supporting employee development and enabling workers to upskill or reskill without having to leave their current positions.

Despite the tremendous benefits of e-learning platforms, challenges remain. Access to high-speed internet and digital devices is essential for effective online learning, and this can be a barrier for students in low-income households or remote regions. Additionally, the effectiveness of online education compared to in-person classes remains a topic of debate among educators and learners alike. While e-learning platforms continue to innovate, adding features like live sessions, virtual labs, and AI-driven tutoring, questions about the depth and quality of learning remain. Nevertheless, e-learning platforms continue to grow, breaking down educational barriers and providing millions of learners with the opportunity to engage in an inclusive, accessible, and global learning environment that expands far beyond the constraints of traditional education systems.

The Flipped Classroom and Blended Learning: New Approaches to Teaching

The flipped classroom model and blended learning represent innovative approaches that are redefining the traditional education model and placing a greater emphasis on student-centered learning. The flipped classroom inverts the traditional structure of teaching, with students studying new material independently at home—often through video lectures or interactive reading assignments and then engaging in practical, collaborative activities in class. This approach not only empowers students to take control of their own learning pace but also enables teachers to use valuable class time for in-depth discussions, problem-solving activities, and personalized support. By shifting the focus from passive to active learning, the flipped classroom cultivates critical thinking, teamwork, and real-world problem-solving skills, which are essential for success in the 21st century.

Blended learning combines online and offline instructional methods, allowing students to benefit from both face-to-face interaction and the flexibility of digital resources. In a blended classroom, for example, students might complete online modules at their own pace outside of school, allowing in-class sessions to focus on collaborative projects or one-on-one interactions with teachers. This hybrid approach is becoming increasingly popular in higher education and in K-12 settings as schools adopt digital tools to support personalized learning. Blended learning can address diverse learning styles by offering a variety of instructional methods, thereby creating an inclusive learning environment where students can thrive regardless of their preferred learning style. It also allows teachers to use data collected from online platforms to monitor student progress, identify areas where individual students may need additional support, and adjust their teaching strategies accordingly.

These approaches have fundamentally altered the role of the teacher, transforming educators from mere providers of information into facilitators of learning. Teachers in flipped or blended classrooms spend less time lecturing and more time supporting students in hands-on activities, answering questions, and providing feedback. This shift allows teachers to cater to individual learning needs, fostering an environment where students actively participate in their own education. By encouraging students to take responsibility for their learning outside the classroom, these models also foster self-discipline, time management, and independent thinking, skills that are crucial for success both academically and professionally.

However, implementing flipped and blended learning models comes with challenges. Teachers need training to design engaging, effective digital content and to manage classroom dynamics in an interactive setting. Developing digital resources requires time and technical skills, and educators may need support in the form of professional development or instructional design teams. Moreover, access to reliable technology and internet connectivity is crucial for students, and without these resources, some learners may struggle to participate fully. Despite these hurdles, the flipped classroom and blended learning are transforming education by creating a more engaging, flexible, and student-centered experience that prepares learners for the demands of an interconnected, technology-driven world.

Artificial Intelligence and Adaptive Learning: Personalizing Education for Every Student

Artificial intelligence (AI) and adaptive learning platforms have introduced a new era of personalized education, allowing teachers and digital platforms to cater to the unique needs of each student based on their individual learning profiles. Adaptive learning technologies use AI algorithms to assess a student's strengths, weaknesses, and learning pace, customizing the curriculum to suit each learner. For example, an adaptive math program may provide extra practice on complex topics for students who struggle, while moving quickly through easier topics they have already mastered. This approach reduces frustration for students by allowing them to engage with material that is appropriately challenging, enhancing learning efficiency and promoting deeper understanding.

AI-powered tools are particularly beneficial in large classrooms where it is difficult for teachers to give individualized attention to every student. AI systems function as virtual tutors, providing students with instant feedback, hints, and explanations as they work through lessons. Adaptive learning platforms such as DreamBox Learning and Knewton are already being used in K-12 and higher education settings to support subjects like mathematics, reading, and science. These platforms collect and analyze real-time data about students' interactions with the material, enabling continuous adjustment to the content and format of instruction. The detailed analytics provided by these systems also allow teachers to identify common areas of difficulty, understand learning patterns, and provide additional support where needed.

AI's applications in education extend beyond adaptive learning. Automated grading systems now assist teachers in assessing student work, saving time and allowing them to focus more on teaching. AI can grade multiple-choice exams, essays, and even complex mathematical problems, offering consistency and efficiency. Chatbots are also being deployed to answer students' questions outside of class hours, providing them with support whenever they need it. In higher education, AI-driven predictive analytics help identify students at risk of falling behind, enabling educators to intervene early with additional resources or personalized support.

However, the use of AI in education raises important ethical and privacy considerations. As AI systems analyze extensive data about students' behavior, performance, and preferences, safeguarding students' privacy becomes a critical concern. Additionally, there is a risk that AI systems may unintentionally reinforce biases if they are not trained on diverse datasets. Ensuring that AI in education is implemented responsibly requires transparency, data protection, and a commitment to unbiased algorithms. While challenges remain, the potential of AI to provide a tailored, adaptive learning experience marks a revolutionary shift in education, promising a future where each student can learn in a way that suits their unique needs, strengths, and aspirations.

Bridging the Digital Divide: Ensuring Equitable Access to Technology in Education

While digital technology has the potential to transform education, the digital divide remains a major obstacle that prevents many students from accessing these benefits. The digital divide refers to the gap between those who have access to digital tools such as computers, tablets, and reliable internet and those who do not. This disparity is particularly stark in low-income communities, rural areas, and developing nations, where infrastructure may be lacking, and families may not have the resources to provide their children with the necessary devices or internet access. For students without these tools, the benefits of digital education remain out of reach, exacerbating existing inequalities in educational outcomes and limiting opportunities for social mobility.

Efforts to bridge the digital divide are crucial for promoting educational equity. Some governments, schools, and non-profit organizations are working to provide devices and internet access to underserved students. For instance, initiatives such as the U.S. Federal Communications Commission's E-Rate program help fund internet access in schools, while programs like One Laptop per Child aim to provide low-cost laptops to students in developing countries. In regions where connectivity is limited, alternative methods are being explored, such as offline learning apps that allow students to access educational content without an internet connection, or community learning centers that provide shared technology resources. These strategies are essential to ensuring that students in underserved areas have opportunities to engage with digital learning resources.

In addition to providing access to technology, bridging the digital divide requires a focus on digital literacy. Digital literacy encompasses the skills needed to use technology effectively, responsibly, and safely. Students must learn not only how to operate devices and navigate online platforms but also how to evaluate information critically, understand digital security, and communicate effectively in virtual environments. Without these skills, students may struggle to fully engage with digital learning and may be more vulnerable to online risks. Many schools are incorporating digital literacy programs into their curricula, teaching students' essential skills that will serve them both academically and professionally.

Teachers play a key role in addressing the digital divide within the classroom. Educators are finding creative ways to include both online and offline resources to ensure that all students can participate in learning activities. For example, teachers may use a combination of printed worksheets, offline digital resources, and interactive activities that do not require internet access, enabling students to continue learning even if they do not have connectivity at home. Educators are also working to foster an inclusive environment by adapting their teaching methods to accommodate students with varying levels of access to technology.

While bridging the digital divide is a complex and ongoing challenge, it is essential for creating an inclusive educational system that offers equal opportunities for all students. As society becomes increasingly dependent on digital technology, ensuring that every student has access to the resources, tools, and skills needed for digital learning will be critical to promoting equity in education. By investing in digital infrastructure, providing affordable devices, and prioritizing digital literacy, we can help all students succeed in a technology-driven world, ensuring that no one is left behind in the digital age.

NURUDEEN D. NURUDEEN

CHAPTER 4
The Future of Work and Automation

The nature of work is undergoing a significant transformation, driven largely by advancements in technology and automation. As machines and algorithms become more capable of performing tasks that were once the exclusive domain of humans, the future of work is being reshaped in profound ways. This chapter explores the impact of automation on the workforce, the challenges and opportunities it presents, and the strategies that individuals and organizations can adopt to navigate this new landscape. The changes we are witnessing are not just about technology; they are about a fundamental shift in how we think about work, productivity, and human potential.

Automation has been a driving force in the evolution of work for centuries, from the Industrial Revolution to the advent of computers and robotics. However, the pace of automation has accelerated dramatically in recent years, thanks to advances in artificial intelligence (AI), machine learning (ML), and robotics. Today, machines are capable of performing a wide range of tasks, from manufacturing and logistics to data analysis and customer service. This has led to increased efficiency and productivity, but it has also raised concerns about job displacement and the future of employment. The potential for automation to disrupt traditional job roles and industries is immense, and the implications for workers, employers, and society as a whole are far-reaching.

One of the most significant impacts of automation is the potential for job displacement. As machines take over routine and repetitive tasks, there is a growing concern that many jobs could become obsolete. This is particularly true in industries such as manufacturing, where automation has already replaced many manual jobs. However, the impact of automation is not limited to low-skill jobs; increasingly, AI and ML are being used to perform tasks that require cognitive skills, such as data analysis, legal research, and even medical diagnostics. The potential for automation to disrupt white-collar jobs is a growing concern, as it challenges the traditional notion that education and skill development are the keys to job security.

While the potential for job displacement is real, it is important to recognize that automation also creates new opportunities. As certain jobs become obsolete, new jobs are emerging in fields such as AI development, data science, and cybersecurity.

Moreover, automation has the potential to free up workers from mundane tasks, allowing them to focus on more creative and strategic work. This shift towards more meaningful and fulfilling work is often referred to as the "automation dividend." The challenge for workers and employers is to ensure that the benefits of automation are shared equitably and that workers are supported in transitioning to new roles and industries.

To navigate the challenges and opportunities presented by automation, individuals and organizations must adopt a proactive approach. For individuals, this means embracing lifelong learning and staying adaptable to changes in the job market. As certain skills become less valuable, workers will need to continually update their skillsets and acquire new competencies to remain competitive. This may involve pursuing further education, gaining certifications in emerging fields, or developing soft skills such as creativity, critical thinking, and emotional intelligence. The ability to adapt to change and to continue learning throughout one's career will be critical to success in an automated world.

Organizations, too, must adapt to the changing landscape of work. This involves rethinking traditional job roles and structures, embracing flexible work arrangements, and investing in employee development. Companies that successfully navigate the transition to a more automated workforce will be those that prioritize innovation, agility, and a commitment to their employees' growth and well-being. This may include reskilling and upskilling programs, as well as creating new roles that complement the capabilities of machines. The ability to integrate human and machine capabilities in a way that maximizes productivity and innovation will be a key differentiator for organizations in the future.

Another important consideration is the ethical implications of automation. As machines take on more responsibilities, questions arise about accountability, fairness, and the potential for bias in decision-making. For example, AI algorithms that are used to make hiring decisions or determine creditworthiness can perpetuate existing biases if they are not carefully designed and monitored. It is crucial for organizations to address these ethical challenges by implementing transparent and fair practices, as well as ensuring that human oversight remains a key component of automated systems. The ethical implications of automation are not just a technical issue; they are a societal issue, and they require careful consideration and thoughtful action.

The future of work is also likely to see a shift towards more flexible and remote working arrangements. The COVID-19 pandemic has accelerated this trend, with many organizations adopting remote work as a long-term strategy. Technology has enabled workers to collaborate and communicate from anywhere in the world, breaking down geographic barriers and creating new opportunities for global talent. However, this shift also presents challenges, such as maintaining team cohesion and ensuring equitable access to remote work opportunities. The ability to manage and support a remote workforce will be a critical skill for managers and leaders in the future of work.

As we look to the future, it is clear that automation will continue to play a central role in shaping the workforce. While the changes it brings may be disruptive, they also offer the potential for a more dynamic, innovative, and inclusive economy. By embracing the opportunities and addressing the challenges, we can create a future of work that benefits everyone. The future of work is not just about technology; it is about people, and about ensuring that everyone has the opportunity to thrive in a rapidly changing world.

The potential of automation to transform work is enormous, but realizing this potential will require careful planning, investment, and a focus on ethical considerations. As we move forward, it is essential to ensure that the benefits of automation are shared by all, and that technology is used to enhance, rather than replace, human capabilities. The future of work is bright, but it is up to us to ensure that it is also equitable, sustainable, and centered on the needs of workers.

Automation and Job Displacement: Navigating the Changing Job Market

The integration of automation into the workplace presents a dual reality characterized by both opportunity and significant challenges. Automation's potential for displacing jobs has become one of the most pressing issues as industries incorporate advanced technologies into their workflows. Historically, technological advancements have led to shifts in labor demands, with certain roles declining while new ones emerged. The Industrial Revolution, for instance, replaced numerous manual jobs but simultaneously introduced new opportunities in factory work, engineering, and management. Today, as automation progresses at an accelerated pace, we're witnessing a similar transition where machines and algorithms increasingly take on tasks once solely performed by humans, resulting in both optimism and apprehension about the future of work.

Currently, routine and repetitive tasks are most vulnerable to automation. Industries ranging from manufacturing and assembly lines to data entry and logistics are witnessing shifts, as AI-driven machines and robotic systems take over these traditionally manual jobs. However, automation's influence is expanding beyond physical labor to white-collar professions as well. AI and ML algorithms are now assisting with data analysis, legal research, and even medical diagnostics, blurring the line between roles requiring human cognitive abilities and those that machines can perform. This development challenges the longstanding belief that higher education and skill development guarantee job security, calling into question the future stability of many traditional careers and creating anxiety about long-term employment.

The phenomenon known as the "automation dividend" presents a more optimistic view of automation, highlighting how delegating repetitive tasks to machines can free human workers for creative, strategic, and meaningful work. When machines handle monotonous responsibilities, employees can focus on tasks requiring critical thinking, problem-solving, and innovation. For businesses, this shift provides an opportunity to reimagine roles, combining the strengths of both humans and machines to optimize efficiency, creativity, and engagement. For instance, in customer service, automated systems handle routine inquiries, allowing representatives to focus on complex cases requiring empathy and nuanced problem-solving.

In addressing the workforce disruption caused by automation, governments, educational institutions, and private organizations each play essential roles. Policymakers can help establish social safety nets and incentives to support reskilling and upskilling programs, ensuring that displaced workers can find new roles in emerging industries. Educational institutions must ensure their curricula remain responsive to the changing job market, equipping students with in-demand skills, such as data science, digital literacy, and artificial intelligence. Simultaneously, private sector organizations can invest in ongoing training and professional development, providing workers with opportunities to transition into future roles within their companies. Through a coordinated approach that balances technological innovation with workforce adaptability, society can harness the benefits of automation while safeguarding against its potential downsides.

New Opportunities in the Age of Automation: Creating Value and Innovation

While automation has the potential to disrupt many existing roles, it also creates vast opportunities for growth, innovation, and new career paths across diverse industries. The rise of specialized fields, such as AI development, data science, robotics engineering, and cybersecurity, underscores the positive impact of automation on modern job markets. These roles demand specialized knowledge, often leading to rewarding, high-paying career opportunities that drive advancements in technology and innovation. As companies implement automation solutions, they require skilled professionals to manage, oversee, and refine these systems, thus expanding job prospects in high-tech and data-driven sectors.

Furthermore, automation encourages a work environment focused on creativity and innovation. With repetitive tasks handled by machines, employees can direct their energy toward strategic projects that leverage human skills such as critical thinking, empathy, and problem-solving. In healthcare, for example, automation alleviates administrative burdens, enabling healthcare professionals to dedicate more time to personalized patient care. Similarly, customer service representatives, free from basic inquiries handled by chatbots, can invest in more meaningful client interactions, enhancing customer relationships and satisfaction. By promoting a shift toward roles that emphasize human abilities, automation can foster a culture of continuous improvement, ingenuity, and strategic planning within organizations.

Automation's impact also extends to entrepreneurship, offering startups and small-to-medium-sized enterprises (SMEs) new opportunities to compete on a global scale. With access to affordable, scalable automation tools, SMEs can reduce operational costs, streamline processes, and enhance the customer experience. Automation allows these businesses to expand into new markets, innovate rapidly, and improve service delivery without the need for large-scale hiring. For instance, e-commerce startups can implement automated systems to manage logistics, inventory, and customer interactions, which previously would have required considerable resources and personnel. As automation technologies become more accessible, these entrepreneurial benefits foster economic growth and drive innovation across various sectors.

Beyond new roles and entrepreneurial benefits, automation has the potential to address industry-specific workforce shortages. Sectors such as agriculture, healthcare, and logistics often struggle to meet workforce demands due to aging populations and increasing workloads. Automation can help bridge these gaps by performing essential tasks traditionally dependent on human labor. In agriculture, for example, automated machines can handle labor-intensive harvesting processes, reducing physical strain on workers and increasing efficiency. In the logistics industry, robotic systems and AI-driven software manage inventory, track orders, and optimize supply chains, enabling companies to meet the demands of a growing e-commerce sector. Through automation, industries experiencing workforce shortages can meet demands while creating opportunities for existing employees to focus on higher-level responsibilities.

Ethical Implications of Automation: Ensuring Fairness and Accountability

Automation's rise brings with it profound ethical considerations, particularly as AI systems take on decision-making roles that affect individuals' lives in tangible ways. As organizations integrate AI into their operations, questions surrounding accountability, bias, and transparency become increasingly relevant. For instance, AI-driven systems used in hiring, lending, and criminal justice must be scrutinized for bias to prevent discrimination and ensure fairness. If an algorithm reflects historical biases present in the data it was trained on, it may inadvertently replicate or even amplify these patterns, thereby perpetuating societal inequalities. This challenge underscores the need for ethical oversight and regulation to ensure AI applications are fair and equitable.

Algorithmic bias is one of the most pressing ethical issues tied to automation, as AI systems learn from vast datasets that may contain historical biases. A hiring algorithm trained on past recruitment data, for example, could disadvantage certain demographics if biases exist in the original data. Addressing algorithmic bias requires careful attention to the data used in training, as well as rigorous testing and auditing. Diverse training data, continuous monitoring, and transparency in algorithm design are essential for minimizing the risk of discrimination and ensuring that automated decisions do not reinforce systemic biases. Organizations have a responsibility to ensure fairness and equal treatment when deploying AI in high-stakes areas.

Accountability is another critical consideration in automation. With machines increasingly involved in decision-making, questions of liability become complex. For example, if an autonomous vehicle malfunctions and causes an accident, responsibility could lie with the manufacturer, software developers, or the vehicle owner. Determining accountability in such scenarios requires clear legal frameworks and industry standards that delineate responsibility and liability in cases involving automated systems. By establishing these guidelines, organizations and governments can foster trust in automation while ensuring that mechanisms are in place to address any unintended consequences or adverse outcomes.

Transparency is also vital for building public trust in automated systems. When AI systems are used to make significant decisions in areas such as healthcare, finance, or law enforcement, affected individuals deserve to understand the factors driving those decisions. This includes the development of "explainable AI" that provides insight into algorithmic processes and decision-making criteria. For example, in criminal justice, transparency can help prevent discriminatory practices by ensuring that predictive policing algorithms are used responsibly and ethically. Implementing transparency and accountability standards enables organizations to harness the benefits of automation while upholding ethical principles and building confidence among users.

Embracing Remote Work and Flexibility: Preparing for a More Agile Workforce

The shift toward remote work has transformed traditional notions of the workplace, offering flexibility, reduced geographic constraints, and a broader talent pool. During the COVID-19 pandemic, remote work became a widespread necessity, with organizations worldwide adopting flexible work arrangements. As digital collaboration tools have advanced, remote work has proven viable and productive, prompting many companies to consider it as a long-term strategy. Employees benefit from enhanced work-life balance, autonomy, and the ability to work in personalized environments, contributing to job satisfaction and well-being. For many, remote work has redefined the workplace, empowering workers with greater control over their professional lives.

From an organizational perspective, remote work has removed geographic limitations on hiring, enabling companies to source top talent from around the world. Knowledge-based industries, in particular, have thrived in remote settings, allowing businesses to access specialized skills regardless of location. Companies are no longer confined to local talent pools, which has been transformative for fields such as technology, finance, and consulting. Additionally, remote work has led to significant cost savings, as companies reduce expenditures on office spaces, utilities, and maintenance. By reallocating these resources, organizations can invest in other areas, such as employee development, digital infrastructure, and innovation, ultimately enhancing their competitiveness and resilience.

However, the transition to remote work presents several challenges, including maintaining team cohesion, fostering communication across time zones, and ensuring fair access to resources. Remote work requires intentional efforts to cultivate a sense of community among distributed teams, such as regular virtual meetings, team-building activities, and open channels of communication. Managers must also develop new skills for remote leadership, including virtual performance management, providing feedback, and supporting team members from afar. Ensuring that employees feel valued and connected to organizational goals is essential for maintaining morale and productivity in remote settings.

Inclusivity is an essential aspect of successful remote work policies, as not all employees have equal access to technology, reliable internet, or a dedicated workspace at home. Organizations can address these disparities by offering resources, such as stipends for office equipment, access to co-working spaces, or flexible work hours. Companies should also prioritize cybersecurity and data privacy to protect sensitive information, as employees work from diverse locations. By addressing the logistical, technological, and ethical considerations of remote work, organizations can create an inclusive environment that accommodates diverse employee needs.

With the right support, remote work has the potential to create a more agile, resilient, and globally interconnected workforce. As companies embrace remote and flexible work arrangements, they can foster a culture of innovation and adaptability, positioning themselves to thrive in a rapidly evolving digital landscape.

NURUDEEN D. NURUDEEN

CHAPTER 5
Smart Cities and Urban Development

The concept of smart cities represents a bold vision for the future of urban living, where technology is seamlessly integrated into the fabric of city life to enhance the quality of life for residents. As urbanization continues to accelerate, with more people living in cities than ever before, the need for innovative solutions to the challenges of urban development has become increasingly urgent. This chapter explores the role of technology in shaping the cities of the future, focusing on the key innovations that are transforming urban environments into smart, sustainable, and connected communities. The transformation of cities into smart cities is not just about technology; it is about reimagining how we live, work, and interact in urban environments.

At the heart of the smart city concept is the idea of using technology to improve the efficiency, sustainability, and livability of urban areas. This involves the integration of digital infrastructure, data analytics, and the Internet of Things (IoT) to create a connected urban environment where everything from traffic management to energy consumption can be optimized in real-time. The goal is to create cities that are not only more efficient and sustainable but also more responsive to the needs and preferences of their residents. Smart cities are about creating environments where technology enhances the quality of life, where services are tailored to the needs of individuals, and where sustainability is a core principle of urban development.

One of the most visible aspects of smart cities is the use of IoT technology to monitor and manage urban infrastructure. IoT sensors can be embedded in roads, bridges, buildings, and other infrastructure to collect data on everything from traffic flow to air quality. This data can then be analyzed in real-time to optimize the operation of the city's systems. For example, smart traffic management systems can use real-time data to adjust traffic signals, reduce congestion, and improve the flow of vehicles. Similarly, smart energy grids can optimize the distribution of electricity, reducing waste and improving the reliability of the power supply. The ability to monitor and manage urban systems in real-time is a key feature of smart cities, enabling them to be more responsive and efficient.

Another important aspect of smart cities is the use of data analytics to inform urban planning and decision-making. By collecting and analyzing data on everything from population density to public transportation usage, city planners can make more informed decisions about where to build new infrastructure, how to allocate resources, and how to improve the overall quality of life for residents. Data-driven urban planning can also help cities become more resilient to challenges such as climate change, by identifying areas that are vulnerable to flooding, heatwaves, or other environmental risks. The ability to use data to inform decisions and to anticipate and respond to challenges is a key advantage of smart cities.

Smart cities also have the potential to improve public services and enhance the quality of life for residents. For example, smart waste management systems can use sensors to monitor the fill levels of trash bins and optimize collection routes, reducing costs and improving the efficiency of waste disposal. Similarly, smart public transportation systems can provide real-time information to passengers, helping them plan their journeys more effectively and reducing wait times. In addition, smart city technologies can be used to improve public safety, by using data analytics to identify crime hotspots and deploy resources more effectively. The ability to use technology to enhance public services and improve the quality of life is a key benefit of smart cities.

The development of smart cities is also closely linked to the concept of sustainability. As cities around the world grapple with the challenges of climate change, pollution, and resource scarcity, there is a growing need for solutions that can reduce the environmental impact of urban living. Smart cities offer a range of tools and technologies that can help cities become more sustainable, from energy-efficient buildings to renewable energy systems. For example, smart buildings can use IoT sensors to monitor energy usage and automatically adjust heating, cooling, and lighting systems to reduce energy consumption. Similarly, smart water management systems can optimize the use of water resources, reducing waste and improving the efficiency of water distribution. The ability to use technology to promote sustainability and reduce the environmental impact of urban living is a key advantage of smart cities.

However, the development of smart cities also raises important challenges and considerations. One of the biggest challenges is the issue of data privacy and security. As cities collect and analyze vast amounts of data on their residents, there is a risk that this data could be misused or fall into the wrong hands. Ensuring that smart city technologies are designed with robust privacy protections and security measures is essential to maintaining public trust and safeguarding the rights of residents. The challenge of protecting data privacy and security is particularly acute in smart cities, where the amount and variety of data collected are vast.

Another challenge is the need to ensure that smart city technologies are accessible and inclusive. As cities become more technologically advanced, there is a risk that certain groups of people, such as the elderly or those with disabilities, may be left behind. It is important to design smart city technologies in a way that is inclusive and accessible to all residents, ensuring that everyone can benefit from the advancements in urban

living. The ability to create inclusive and accessible environments is a key challenge for smart cities, and it requires careful planning and a commitment to equity.

The development of smart cities is still in its early stages, but the potential benefits are enormous. By leveraging technology to create more efficient, sustainable, and responsive urban environments, we can improve the quality of life for millions of people around the world. As we continue to develop and implement smart city technologies, it will be important to address the challenges and ensure that these innovations are used in a way that benefits all residents and creates a more equitable and sustainable future. The future of smart cities is bright, but it is up to us to ensure that it is also inclusive, equitable, and centered on the needs of residents.

The potential of smart cities to transform urban living is enormous, but realizing this potential will require careful planning, investment, and a focus on ethical considerations. As we move forward, it is essential to ensure that the benefits of smart cities are shared by all, and that technology is used to enhance, rather than replace, the human elements of urban life. The future of cities is bright, but it is up to us to ensure that it is also sustainable, equitable, and centered on the needs of residents.

IoT and Infrastructure: Real-Time Management for Efficient Cities

The Internet of Things (IoT) stands as a transformative force in the evolution of smart cities, with its potential to monitor and manage vast urban ecosystems in real-time, fundamentally changing how cities operate. By integrating IoT sensors into roads, buildings, utilities, and public spaces, cities can collect a wealth of data on environmental conditions, infrastructure health, public safety, and resource usage. This data enables city officials to make precise adjustments in real-time, enhancing the efficiency and responsiveness of municipal operations. For example, IoT-enabled traffic systems dynamically adjust traffic lights to ease congestion during peak hours, shortening commute times, reducing emissions, and alleviating the stress of gridlock for drivers. Cities like Los Angeles and Singapore have successfully implemented these traffic systems, significantly enhanced urban mobility and minimized the environmental impact of traffic.

IoT technology also brings substantial improvements to essential services like waste management, water conservation, and energy distribution. Waste management systems, equipped with smart sensors, track waste levels in bins, alerting collection services only when bins are near capacity. This data-driven approach reduces collection trips, saving fuel and lowering operational costs while minimizing emissions from waste trucks. In water-scarce cities, IoT-based water management systems monitor usage patterns, detect leaks, and regulate distribution, conserving water and reducing wastage. These systems are especially valuable in drought-prone regions, where water conservation is critical to urban resilience. By reducing resource wastage, smart waste and water management systems help cities operate more sustainably and responsibly.

Public safety is also transformed by IoT. Connected surveillance cameras, smart streetlights, and IoT-enabled emergency response systems create a secure urban environment. Smart streetlights, for example, automatically adjust brightness based on pedestrian or vehicle activity, reducing energy consumption while providing safer nighttime visibility. In emergency situations, IoT devices such as smoke detectors and security cameras can instantly alert authorities, improving response times. In cases of fire or medical emergencies, IoT technology facilitates quicker intervention by sending detailed, location-specific information to first responders, potentially saving lives. Overall, IoT-driven infrastructure management not only improves city efficiency but also enhances the safety, sustainability, and quality of life for all residents. The integration of IoT within city infrastructure is not just a technological leap; it represents a new paradigm in urban living, where cities can better understand and respond to the needs of their communities.

Data-Driven Urban Planning: Designing Cities for Tomorrow

Data-driven urban planning is reshaping the way cities grow, adapt, and address emerging challenges, allowing for proactive and evidence-based decisions that ensure cities can sustainably meet future needs. Traditional urban planning was typically reactive, guided by historical data and long-term projections that could often fall short as cities evolved. In contrast, modern urban planning leverages real-time data from a variety of sources, including IoT sensors, public records, and satellite imagery, offering a comprehensive understanding of city dynamics. This data-driven approach enables planners to address the immediate needs of residents while preparing for future growth, optimizing city layouts, transit systems, and resource distribution. Data on public transportation usage, for example, allows planners to adjust routes and schedules dynamically, ensuring that public transit is reliable and accessible to all neighborhoods. This optimizes service delivery, reduces road congestion, and encourages greater use of sustainable transportation.

Moreover, data analysis enables cities to make informed decisions regarding land use, housing, and green spaces, balancing population density with the need for recreation areas and environmental considerations. In growing cities, data on housing trends, economic activity, and demographic changes can help predict where new infrastructure and public services are needed most, allowing for more equitable development. By analyzing pedestrian and cycling patterns, cities can also create safe, accessible paths that encourage residents to adopt healthier, eco-friendly transportation modes. Cities like Barcelona and Amsterdam have used data-driven planning to increase walkability and bike-friendliness, improving residents' quality of life while reducing vehicular traffic and pollution.

Data-driven planning is equally essential for building resilience against climate change. Predictive analytics enable cities to prepare for extreme weather events by identifying vulnerable zones and reinforcing infrastructure. For example, data on flooding risks can guide the construction of flood barriers, while heat mapping can inform the development of cooling centers and green roofs in densely populated areas. In places like Miami and Rotterdam, data-driven resilience planning has led to significant investments in flood defenses and urban cooling solutions, protecting residents and enhancing urban adaptability. By fostering cities that are not only prepared for current demands but also resilient to future challenges, data-driven planning supports sustainable urban growth that aligns with the needs of both residents and the environment.

Enhancing Public Services: Technology for a Better Quality of Life

Smart cities strive to enhance the quality of life for residents by improving essential services like public transportation, waste management, energy distribution, and public safety. Through technology, cities are creating a seamless urban experience where these services operate more efficiently and adapt to residents' needs. For instance, real-time data in public transit systems provides commuters with accurate updates on arrival and departure times, allowing them to better plan their journeys and reduce wait times. In cities like London and Seoul, where transit systems integrate digital payment solutions, commuters benefit from a streamlined, user-friendly experience, which encourages the use of public transport over private vehicles. By improving public transit accessibility and efficiency, smart cities reduce congestion, cut emissions, and make daily commuting more pleasant.

In waste management, IoT sensors in trash bins monitor fill levels and notify waste collection teams when bins are full, optimizing collection routes and minimizing unnecessary trips.

This approach saves fuel, reduces vehicle emissions, and allows collection teams to focus on high-demand areas, contributing to both economic and environmental efficiency. Similarly, smart energy grids improve the resilience and sustainability of urban power systems by monitoring real-time energy demand and adjusting distribution accordingly. During peak usage times, smart grids can prioritize energy flow to critical areas, ensuring uninterrupted access to essential services. In California and parts of Australia, smart grids have proven invaluable during extreme weather conditions, allowing cities to maintain stable power supplies in the face of increased demand.

Public safety also benefits from technological integration. Predictive analytics allow law enforcement agencies to anticipate crime trends, allocate resources effectively, and maintain safer neighborhoods. Smart lighting systems, which adjust brightness in response to pedestrian traffic, provide safer, well-lit areas for evening commuters while conserving energy. Additionally, IoT-connected emergency response systems enable faster, more efficient incident management by notifying authorities in real-time. When combined, these smart city services create a safer, more responsive urban environment that enhances residents' quality of life. By focusing on how people interact with their city daily, smart cities create an urban experience that is not only more efficient but also more supportive of community well-being, making city life both convenient and secure.

Building for Sustainability: Green Infrastructure and Resource Management

In an era of climate change and environmental challenges, sustainable urban development has become essential, and smart cities are leading the way with green infrastructure and resource-efficient practices. At the center of this shift are smart buildings equipped with IoT sensors and eco-friendly systems that optimize resource use. These buildings adjust lighting, heating, and cooling based on occupancy levels and weather conditions, substantially reducing energy waste. Features like green roofs, solar panels, and rainwater harvesting systems further minimize environmental impact, lowering utility costs and contributing to the city's overall sustainability goals. Cities such as San Francisco and Copenhagen have embraced these green building standards, resulting in urban spaces that are healthier for residents and less taxing on natural resources.

Beyond buildings, water management is another priority for sustainable city development. Smart water systems equipped with IoT sensors monitor real-time water usage, detect leaks, and control distribution, reducing water waste and ensuring equitable access across neighborhoods. In cities like Cape Town, which has faced severe droughts, these systems have proven critical for managing limited water resources and preventing shortages. Additionally, cities are implementing rainwater harvesting, wastewater recycling, and desalination technologies to supplement traditional water sources, making urban water supplies more resilient. By integrating sustainable water practices, smart cities promote resource conservation and prepare for future population growth without overburdening natural water reserves.

Transportation infrastructure in sustainable cities also reflects a commitment to reducing emissions and promoting eco-friendly mobility. Electric vehicle (EV) charging stations, bike-sharing programs, and pedestrian pathways are all part of a transportation ecosystem that encourages cleaner commuting options. In cities like Oslo, where EV infrastructure is extensive, residents are increasingly choosing electric vehicles, significantly reducing air pollution. Smart city technology further enhances sustainable mobility by providing real-time data on transit options, carpool availability, and optimal walking routes, reducing reliance on fossil fuel-powered vehicles. By creating integrated, eco-friendly transportation networks, smart cities not only reduce their carbon footprint but also foster healthier lifestyles for residents. As urban populations grow, the emphasis on green infrastructure and sustainable practices will become even more vital, ensuring that cities can thrive economically and socially without compromising environmental health.

CHAPTER 6
Technology's Role in Environmental Sustainability

Environmental sustainability is one of the most pressing challenges of our time, and technology has a critical role to play in addressing this challenge. As the global population continues to grow and industrialization accelerates, the strain on our planet's natural resources has reached unprecedented levels. The need for sustainable solutions has never been more urgent, and technology offers powerful tools for addressing the environmental challenges we face. In this chapter, we explore the ways in which technology is being used to promote environmental sustainability, from renewable energy and smart agriculture to waste management and conservation efforts. These innovations are not just about reducing our impact on the planet; they are about reimagining how we live, work, and interact with the environment.

One of the most significant ways in which technology is contributing to environmental sustainability is through the development of renewable energy sources. Renewable energy technologies, such as solar, wind, and hydropower, offer a sustainable alternative to fossil fuels, which are a major contributor to greenhouse gas emissions and climate change. Advances in technology have made renewable energy more efficient and cost-effective, leading to widespread adoption around the world. For example, the cost of solar panels has decreased dramatically in recent years, making solar power a viable option for homes and businesses alike. Similarly, advances in wind turbine technology have increased the efficiency and reliability of wind power, making it a key component of the global energy mix. The transition to renewable energy is a critical part of addressing climate change and reducing our dependence on fossil fuels.

Smart grids are another technological innovation that is helping to promote environmental sustainability. Smart grids use digital technology to monitor and manage the production, distribution, and consumption of electricity in real-time. This allows for more efficient use of energy resources, reducing waste and improving the reliability of the power supply. For example, smart grids can automatically adjust the flow of electricity to match demand, reducing the need for energy-intensive power plants to operate at full capacity. They can also integrate renewable energy sources, such as solar and wind, more effectively into the grid, ensuring that clean energy is used whenever possible. The ability to monitor and manage energy systems in real-time is a key advantage of smart grids, enabling them to be more responsive and efficient.

Technology is also playing a crucial role in the development of sustainable agriculture. As the global population continues to grow, the demand for food is increasing, putting pressure on the world's agricultural systems. To meet this demand while minimizing environmental impact, farmers are turning to technology to improve the efficiency and sustainability of their operations. Precision agriculture, for example, uses GPS, IoT sensors, and data analytics to optimize the use of water, fertilizers, and pesticides, reducing waste and improving crop yields. Similarly, vertical farming and hydroponics use advanced technology to grow crops in controlled environments, reducing the need for land and water while increasing productivity. The ability to use technology to optimize agricultural practices is a key advantage in promoting sustainability and ensuring food security.

In addition to energy and agriculture, technology is also being used to promote environmental sustainability in other areas, such as waste management and conservation. For example, smart waste management systems use IoT sensors to monitor the fill levels of trash bins and optimize collection routes, reducing the environmental impact of waste disposal. Recycling technologies are also improving, with advances in sorting and processing systems that make it easier to recycle a wider range of materials. Conservation efforts are also benefiting from technology, with tools such as drones and satellite imagery being used to monitor wildlife populations and track deforestation, helping to protect endangered species and preserve natural habitats. The ability to use technology to promote conservation and reduce waste is a key advantage in addressing environmental challenges.

However, the use of technology to promote environmental sustainability is not without its challenges. One of the biggest challenges is the issue of resource consumption. While technology can help to reduce the environmental impact of certain activities, the production and use of technology itself can also be resource-intensive. For example, the manufacturing of solar panels and wind turbines requires the extraction and processing of raw materials, which can have negative environmental impacts. Similarly, the production of electronic devices and the infrastructure needed to support smart grids and other technologies can generate significant amounts of e-waste. The challenge of managing the environmental impact of technology is a critical issue that must be addressed to ensure that technology is truly sustainable.

Another challenge is the need for global cooperation and coordination. Environmental sustainability is a global issue that requires a coordinated response from all countries and stakeholders. However, the adoption and implementation of sustainable technologies can vary widely between regions, depending on factors such as economic development, infrastructure, and political will. Ensuring that all countries have access to the technology and resources needed to promote environmental sustainability is essential to achieving global sustainability goals. The ability to coordinate and collaborate on a global scale is a key challenge in promoting sustainability and ensuring that the benefits of technology are shared by all.

Despite these challenges, the potential for technology to contribute to environmental sustainability is immense. By leveraging technological innovations, we can reduce our impact on the planet, protect natural resources, and create a more sustainable future for generations to come. The key will be to ensure that these technologies are developed and implemented in a way that balances the need for economic growth with the imperative to protect the environment. The future of sustainability is bright, but it is up to us to ensure that it is also equitable, inclusive, and centered on the needs of people and the planet.

The potential of technology to transform environmental sustainability is enormous, but realizing this potential will require careful planning, investment, and a focus on ethical considerations. As we move forward, it is essential to ensure that the benefits of sustainability are shared by all, and that technology is used to enhance, rather than replace, our connection to the environment. The future of sustainability is bright, but it is up to us to ensure that it is also equitable, sustainable, and centered on the needs of people and the planet.

Advancements in Renewable Energy: A Path to a Greener Future

Renewable energy technologies such as solar, wind, and hydropower are essential to reducing global reliance on fossil fuels, which are a primary contributor to greenhouse gas emissions and climate change. The significant advancements in solar technology have drastically reduced the cost of solar panels, making solar energy increasingly accessible for residential, commercial, and industrial use. This accessibility has catalyzed widespread adoption, transforming solar energy from a niche alternative into a critical component of the energy landscape. Innovations in photovoltaic cells have not only improved energy capture efficiency but have also expanded solar applications, allowing it to be viable in regions with varying sunlight exposure. Nations like China, the United States, and India are leading global production, demonstrating that large-scale adoption is not only feasible but instrumental in reducing carbon emissions and supporting sustainable development goals.

Similarly, wind energy has witnessed remarkable advancements that enable greater energy output even in low-wind conditions, thanks to innovations in turbine design and materials. New models, such as vertical-axis turbines and floating offshore turbines, allow for expanded installations in diverse locations, including urban and offshore settings where traditional horizontal-axis turbines are less practical. Europe, particularly countries like Germany, Denmark, and the United Kingdom, has invested heavily in offshore wind, creating vast wind farms that collectively produce enough energy to power millions of homes. Additionally, wind farms are increasingly integrating battery storage solutions to offset intermittency, ensuring a reliable supply even when conditions are calm. The confluence of wind and solar power, combined with advanced storage technologies, represents a fundamental shift towards cleaner, sustainable energy networks capable of meeting the demands of a growing population.

Hydropower, one of the oldest and most established forms of renewable energy, continues to play a vital role in the energy transition, especially in regions with abundant water resources. Innovations such as small-scale hydropower and run-of-river systems minimize the ecological disruption traditionally associated with large dams, making hydropower a viable option for smaller communities and areas where large-scale infrastructure would be intrusive. These small systems are increasingly deployed in rural and remote areas, providing localized power that supports both community development and energy independence. While hydropower projects require careful consideration of environmental impacts, such as fish migration and water flow, new technologies like fish-friendly turbines and improved water management strategies aim to minimize these issues, creating a more sustainable way to harness water resources.

The cumulative impact of these renewable energy advancements points to a future where clean energy is not only abundant but also scalable to meet global demands. As countries around the world transition from fossil fuels, renewable energy is proving to be a sustainable alternative that not only mitigates climate change but also fosters economic growth, energy security, and resilience against volatile fuel prices. With ongoing research and development, renewable energy technologies are expected to become even more efficient and cost-effective, enabling wider adoption and making a green energy future a tangible reality.

Smart Grids and Energy Efficiency: Optimizing Resource Use

Smart grid technology is revolutionizing energy management by enabling real-time monitoring, adaptive energy distribution, and efficient integration of renewable resources. Traditional grids operate on a fixed supply system, leading to frequent mismatches between energy production and demand, resulting in waste. In contrast, smart grids use data analytics, AI, and IoT to monitor and predict fluctuations in energy use, facilitating a more responsive system that can adjust to real-time needs. By dynamically distributing resources, smart grids reduce the strain on power plants, decrease energy waste, and improve the reliability of electricity supply to both residential and industrial areas. The ability to prioritize renewable sources, such as wind and solar, on days when they are most abundant demonstrates the profound potential of smart grids to reduce fossil fuel dependency and lower emissions.

One critical component of smart grids is the implementation of smart meters, which provide consumers and utilities with detailed insights into energy usage patterns. Smart meters enable users to monitor their electricity consumption in real-time, empowering households and businesses to adopt more energy-efficient practices. With the integration of time-of-use pricing models, smart meters encourage users to shift their energy use to off-peak hours, reducing demand during peak periods and balancing the load on the grid. For instance, many utility companies offer incentives to customers who utilize energy during off-peak times, helping to reduce overall consumption and lower costs for consumers. By fostering greater awareness of energy habits, smart meters contribute to behavioral shifts toward conservation, which can have a lasting impact on energy sustainability.

Additionally, smart grids enable decentralized energy production, allowing consumers to generate and store their own power through solar panels, wind turbines, or other micro-generators. Known as "prosumers," these energy producers reduce the burden on large-scale power plants and create a more resilient grid less vulnerable to outages or disruptions. Battery storage solutions, such as Tesla's Powerwall or larger community-scale batteries, allow households and communities to store surplus energy generated from renewables for later use, providing stability to the grid even during peak demand or emergency situations. Decentralized energy production also creates opportunities for peer-to-peer energy sharing, where surplus energy can be sold or shared with neighbors, fostering a community-centric approach to energy use.

The rise of smart grids represents a transformative shift in energy management, paving the way for a more sustainable, resilient, and efficient energy system. As smart grid technology advances, it will play an increasingly crucial role in integrating renewable sources, optimizing resource use, and empowering consumers to participate actively in energy conservation. The environmental benefits of smart grids are significant, contributing not only to lower emissions and reduced fossil fuel use but also to the creation of adaptable, future-ready energy networks that will support both environmental and economic sustainability.

Sustainable Agriculture: Feeding a Growing Population Responsibly

As the global population approaches 10 billion, sustainable agriculture has become essential for meeting food demand without compromising the planet's health. Agricultural practices are shifting towards sustainability, leveraging technology to increase productivity while conserving resources. Precision agriculture, for example, combines data analytics, satellite imagery, IoT sensors, and GPS to manage crops efficiently and with minimal waste. By analyzing data on soil health, moisture levels, and weather conditions, farmers can optimize water usage, apply fertilizers and pesticides only where needed, and reduce overall input costs. This data-driven approach conserves resources, mitigates environmental damage, and improves crop yields, allowing farmers to meet demand more sustainably. Precision agriculture has proven especially valuable in water-scarce regions, where efficient irrigation can make the difference between success and failure.

Vertical farming and hydroponics are other innovative approaches that redefine traditional agriculture by growing crops in controlled indoor environments. In vertical farms, plants are grown in stacked layers, maximizing space and using up to 90% less water than conventional farming methods. This efficiency is achieved through hydroponics, a soil-free system where nutrients are delivered directly to the plant roots in a water-based solution. By recycling water, hydroponics drastically reduces consumption, making it ideal for arid urban areas where water is limited. These practices allow cities to produce fresh produce locally, reducing the need for long-distance transportation, which contributes to emissions. Cities like Singapore, with limited arable land, are adopting vertical farms, creating a local food supply that minimizes import dependency and cuts down on carbon emissions associated with food transport.

Biotechnology is also making strides in sustainable agriculture, with genetically modified (GM) crops that are designed to withstand drought, pests, and diseases, significantly improving food security and reducing the need for chemical pesticides. While GM crops have been controversial, the latest advances focus on reducing environmental impact by creating plants that require fewer resources to thrive. This includes crops engineered to use less water and fertilizers, which is particularly beneficial in regions facing resource constraints. Furthermore, advancements in CRISPR gene-editing technology enable scientists to develop crop varieties with improved resilience and nutritional content without introducing foreign genes, making these innovations more acceptable to the public.

Through sustainable agriculture practices, we are taking steps to ensure that food production aligns with environmental preservation. By adopting precision farming, hydroponics, and biotechnology, the agricultural sector can contribute to climate resilience, resource conservation, and improved food security, meeting the dietary needs of a growing global population while protecting the planet for future generations.

Conservation and Waste Management: Protecting Natural Resources and Reducing Pollution

Conservation and waste management play pivotal roles in environmental sustainability, with technology providing innovative solutions to safeguard ecosystems and reduce pollution. Conservation efforts are now supported by advanced tools like satellite imagery, drones, and GPS tracking, which allow scientists and environmentalists to monitor ecosystems and wildlife populations remotely. For instance, drones equipped with high-resolution cameras can capture images of vast forests, enabling conservationists to track deforestation, illegal logging, and other activities that threaten biodiversity. Satellite data is equally valuable, offering a macro perspective on land-use changes, such as urban sprawl or agricultural expansion, that affect wildlife habitats. By collecting precise data, conservation organizations can make informed decisions and implement strategies that protect endangered species, restore degraded ecosystems, and preserve natural habitats.

Waste management has also evolved, thanks to IoT-enabled systems that streamline waste collection and promote recycling. Smart waste bins, equipped with sensors, monitor fill levels and communicate with waste collection services, allowing for optimized collection routes that reduce fuel consumption and emissions from waste trucks. This system prevents overflowing bins, minimizes collection frequency, and lowers operational costs, contributing to a cleaner, more efficient urban environment. Additionally, automated sorting systems, powered by AI and machine vision, can efficiently separate recyclable materials from general waste, increasing recycling rates and reducing the need for new raw materials. These systems are instrumental in processing complex waste streams, such as e-waste, which contains valuable metals like gold and copper. By recovering these materials, we reduce demand for mining and decrease the environmental impact associated with extracting new resources.

Electronic waste, or e-waste, has become a critical environmental concern, with rapid technological turnover leading to millions of tons of discarded devices annually. Specialized recycling facilities now use advanced extraction techniques to safely reclaim metals and other components from e-waste, reducing landfill waste and preventing toxic substances from leaching into the soil and water. Public awareness campaigns and take-back programs encourage consumers to recycle electronics responsibly, further mitigating e-waste pollution. E-waste recycling not only conserves valuable materials but also addresses hazardous waste issues, as improper disposal of electronics can release harmful chemicals into the environment.

The combined efforts in conservation and waste management highlight the vital role of technology in promoting environmental sustainability. From conserving biodiversity to reducing landfill waste, these practices ensure a balanced approach to resource use and pollution prevention. By continuing to innovate in waste reduction and conservation, we can protect the natural world while addressing the environmental challenges of modern society, creating a cleaner, more sustainable future for generations to come.

NURUDEEN D. NURUDEEN

CHAPTER 7
The Impact of Social-Media on Society

Social media has evolved into one of the most influential forces in modern society, fundamentally altering the ways in which we communicate, share information, and interact with one another. From its humble beginnings as a platform for personal connections among friends and family, social media has grown into a global phenomenon that shapes public opinion, drives social movements, and influences political outcomes on a massive scale. This chapter delves deeply into the multifaceted impact of social media on society, exploring both its positive and negative effects, and examining how it continues to transform our lives in ways that are both profound and complex.

One of the most significant impacts of social media is its unparalleled ability to connect people across vast distances, effectively bridging geographic, cultural, and social divides. Social media platforms like Facebook, Twitter, Instagram, and TikTok have enabled billions of people to stay in touch with friends, family, and colleagues, fostering a sense of global interconnectedness that was previously unimaginable. This connectivity has created a world where experiences, ideas, and information can be shared instantaneously, breaking down barriers that once limited communication and understanding. In this new social landscape, individuals are not only able to maintain relationships across distances, but they also gain access to a wider range of perspectives and experiences than ever before. Additionally, social media has provided a powerful platform for marginalized and underrepresented communities to amplify their voices, raise awareness about critical issues, and mobilize for change, creating new opportunities for social justice and equity.

The role of social media in social movements and activism is perhaps one of its most impactful contributions to society. Platforms like Twitter and Facebook have become essential tools for organizing protests, raising awareness of social issues, and garnering support for various causes. The #MeToo movement, for instance, gained momentum on social media as women across the globe shared their experiences with sexual harassment and assault, leading to a broader societal reckoning that continues to influence public discourse and policy. Similarly, the Black Lives Matter movement utilized social media to highlight issues of racial inequality and police brutality, sparking widespread protests and calls for systemic change that have reverberated across the world. These movements demonstrate the power of social media to mobilize large groups of people, influence public discourse, and bring about meaningful social change, effectively transforming the landscape of activism and advocacy in the digital age.

In addition to its role in activism, social media has revolutionized the way we consume and disseminate information, fundamentally altering the nature of journalism and media. The rise of social media has democratized access to news and information, allowing anyone with an internet connection to share content with a global audience. This has led to the emergence of citizen journalism, where individuals report on events and share their perspectives in real-time, often bypassing traditional media channels and offering alternative viewpoints that might otherwise be overlooked. Social media has also transformed the relationship between traditional media outlets and their audiences, with many news organizations now using social platforms to distribute content, engage with readers, and gather feedback, thereby creating a more dynamic and interactive media environment.

However, the influence of social media is not without its challenges and drawbacks. One of the most pressing concerns is the proliferation of misinformation and fake news, which has become a pervasive issue in the digital age. The open and unregulated nature of social media platforms makes it easy for false or misleading information to spread rapidly, often with little or no fact-checking or accountability. This has led to the widespread dissemination of conspiracy theories, hoaxes, and misleading content, which can have serious consequences for public health, safety, and democratic processes. For example, misinformation about COVID-19 vaccines has fueled vaccine hesitancy and resistance, undermining efforts to control the pandemic and protect public health. Similarly, misinformation during political campaigns has the potential to distort public perception and influence election outcomes, raising concerns about the integrity of democratic processes in the digital age.

Another significant challenge posed by social media is the issue of online harassment and cyberbullying, which has become a growing concern in recent years. The anonymity and reach of social media platforms have made it easier for individuals to engage in abusive behavior, targeting others with threats, insults, and harassment. This can have devastating effects on the mental health and well-being of victims, leading to anxiety, depression, and, in extreme cases, suicide. Social media companies have faced criticism for their handling of online harassment, with many calling for greater accountability and more effective moderation of harmful content to protect users. The rise of online harassment highlights the darker side of social media, where the same platforms that enable connection and community can also become tools for harm and abuse.

The impact of social media on mental health extends beyond harassment and cyberbullying, affecting users in more subtle but equally significant ways. While social media can foster a sense of connection and community, it can also contribute to feelings of isolation, anxiety, and inadequacy, particularly among young people. The constant exposure to curated images and highlights of other people's lives can create unrealistic expectations and lead to negative self-perception, as users compare themselves to the seemingly perfect lives portrayed online. Research has shown that excessive use of social media is associated with increased levels of anxiety, depression, and loneliness, particularly among adolescents and young adults. The pressure to conform to social norms and the fear of missing out (FOMO) can exacerbate these feelings, creating a cycle of negative emotions that can have long-term consequences for mental health.

Despite these challenges, social media also has the potential to bring about positive change and contribute to the betterment of society. When used responsibly, social media can be a powerful tool for education, awareness, and social good. It provides a platform for important conversations, amplifies underrepresented voices, and brings people together to create positive change in their communities. Social media has been used to raise awareness about environmental issues, promote mental health initiatives, and support charitable causes, demonstrating its potential to be a force for good in the world. For example, social media campaigns have successfully mobilized resources for disaster relief efforts, connected people with support networks during times of crisis, and sparked global movements for social and environmental justice.

As we continue to navigate the complexities of social media, it is crucial to recognize both its potential and its pitfalls. To harness the power of social media for the benefit of society, it is essential to foster a culture of responsible use, promote digital literacy, and hold social media companies accountable for their actions. This includes implementing measures to combat misinformation, protect users from online harassment, and support mental well-being. By doing so, we can ensure that social media enhances, rather than detracts from, our overall well-being and contributes to a more informed, connected, and compassionate world. The future of social media will depend on our collective ability to address its challenges and maximize its benefits, creating a digital environment that is both safe and empowering for all users.

The Power of Global Connectivity: Building Bridges Across Boundaries

Social media has fundamentally transformed global connectivity, enabling individuals to forge meaningful relationships across vast distances and cultural divides. Through platforms like Facebook, Twitter, Instagram, and TikTok, billions of people stay connected with friends, family, and colleagues while accessing a rich diversity of viewpoints and experiences. This accessibility has created a powerful framework for global understanding, fostering relationships that might have once seemed impossible. Moreover, social media provides a vital lifeline for isolated communities, allowing them to connect with the broader world and access essential resources, information, and networks.

In today's interconnected world, social media is not just a tool for personal connections but a platform for learning, professional networking, and cultural exchange. Individuals and communities now have access to educational resources, professional webinars, and career development tools that were previously accessible only through formal institutions. This access is particularly transformative for those in underserved regions, where social media provides an entryway into the global knowledge economy. As a result, people can learn, collaborate, and contribute on a global scale, transcending geographical and socio-economic barriers.

Social media also empowers marginalized communities to amplify their voices and share their stories. Platforms enable these groups to raise awareness and advocate for issues that are often overlooked by mainstream media, from indigenous land rights to LGBTQ+ representation. By providing a space for authentic narratives, social media allows these communities to bypass traditional gatekeepers, reach global audiences, and effect change. This democratization of information has created an unprecedented avenue for social justice, where previously underrepresented voices can now influence public opinion and policy on an international level.

Global connectivity through social media also has significant implications for humanitarian efforts. In times of crisis, platforms are essential for coordinating relief, raising funds, and disseminating life-saving information. Social media allows people to respond quickly to disasters and humanitarian crises, fostering a collective sense of responsibility and solidarity. As a result, communities can unite to provide immediate support, whether through donations, resource sharing, or volunteer recruitment. This digital solidarity reflects the broader power of social media to create a connected, compassionate global community.

Fueling Social Movements and Activism: Catalysts for Change

Social media has fundamentally reshaped the landscape of social and political activism, empowering ordinary people to become agents of change. Movements like #MeToo and Black Lives Matter, which have achieved global prominence, showcase the power of social media to spark worldwide conversations on critical social issues. Through hashtags, posts, and viral videos, these movements have mobilized millions, turning local injustices into global calls for action. The rapid and widespread dissemination of information has made it easier to organize protests, rally supporters, and draw attention to pressing issues, thereby transforming the dynamics of modern activism.

The *#MeToo* movement, for example, exemplified how social media can amplify individual voices to challenge powerful institutions. Through a simple hashtag, survivors of sexual harassment and assault were able to share their stories, creating a global dialogue on issues of gender equality and workplace misconduct. Similarly, the Black Lives Matter movement harnessed social media to highlight racial injustice, raising awareness about systemic inequality and police brutality. These movements are more than digital campaigns; they are tangible social revolutions, facilitated by social media's capacity to unite people around shared values and causes.

Social media has also democratized access to activism, allowing grassroots campaigns to reach global audiences without the need for traditional organizational infrastructure. For environmental movements like #FridaysForFuture, young activists use platforms to mobilize for climate action, share scientific information, and connect with supporters worldwide. This decentralized structure means that anyone, anywhere, can participate in these movements, organizing local events and contributing to a unified global cause. This ease of participation has lowered the barriers to entry for activism, encouraging a diverse range of voices to advocate for issues that matter to them.

Beyond raising awareness, social media serves as a tool for accountability. By providing a platform to document and broadcast events as they unfold, social media holds institutions, governments, and public figures accountable for their actions. During protests and demonstrations, activists can capture and share incidents of police violence or misconduct, sparking public outrage and demanding justice. The immediate and global visibility offered by social media creates a powerful check on authority, ensuring that injustices are documented and addressed in real-time.

The Rise of Citizen Journalism and Media Democratization

Social media has catalyzed the rise of citizen journalism, allowing individuals to document and report on events as they happen. This shift has democratized the media landscape, challenging traditional news outlets as the primary gatekeepers of information. In moments of crisis or social upheaval, ordinary citizens can provide on-the-ground reports that are instantly shared with a global audience, often bypassing the filters and biases of mainstream media. By providing real-time access to unfiltered content, social media offers a diverse array of perspectives, enriching our understanding of complex issues.

The Arab Spring serves as a prominent example of how citizen journalism reshaped global news coverage. During the protests, social media became the primary source of information, with citizens sharing videos, images, and updates directly from the streets. These firsthand accounts provided the world with unprecedented insight into the political climate and struggles faced by protestors, highlighting the power of social media to offer perspectives that traditional news sources might overlook. Citizen journalism has since become a staple in global media, empowering people to share their stories and shape public narratives.

While citizen journalism has expanded access to information, it has also introduced challenges related to misinformation and accountability. Unlike professional journalism, citizen reports are not subject to editorial oversight or fact-checking, which increases the risk of spreading unverified information. During emergencies or contentious events, this unregulated nature can lead to the rapid dissemination of rumors, causing confusion and, at times, panic. However, the rise of citizen journalism underscores the importance of media literacy, as audiences must critically evaluate the reliability and intent of content shared on social platforms.

In response, traditional news organizations have adapted by integrating social media into their reporting practices. Journalists use platforms like Twitter for live updates, while news outlets engage audiences on Instagram and TikTok to attract younger demographics. This fusion of traditional and digital media has created a more dynamic and interactive news environment, where users can engage directly with journalists and contribute to the news cycle. The convergence of citizen and traditional journalism represents a new era of media, one that encourages active participation and fosters a richer, more inclusive discourse.

Misinformation and Fake News: Navigating the Perils of the Digital Age

One of the most significant challenges presented by social media is the proliferation of misinformation and fake news. Unlike traditional media, where content is subject to rigorous editorial standards, social media lacks similar oversight, allowing false information to spread unchecked. Algorithms that prioritize engagement often amplify sensationalized content, further fueling the spread of misinformation. This dynamic can have serious consequences, as misinformation influences public perception, shapes political discourse, and, in extreme cases, jeopardizes public health and safety.

The COVID-19 pandemic illustrated the dangers of misinformation on social media. From false claims about virus origins to conspiracy theories about vaccines, social media became a breeding ground for inaccurate information that undermined public health initiatives. This misinformation created confusion, fueled skepticism, and contributed to vaccine hesitancy, highlighting the urgent need for accountability in content dissemination. The rapid spread of misleading content during the pandemic underscored the responsibility of social media companies to monitor and regulate the information shared on their platforms.

Social media companies have attempted to address misinformation through fact-checking partnerships, content warnings, and algorithm adjustments. However, these measures have sparked debates over censorship and free speech, as critics argue that efforts to curb misinformation could infringe on users' rights to express their opinions. Striking a balance between safeguarding public welfare and preserving free speech remains a contentious issue, underscoring the complexity of managing misinformation in a digital age that values open dialogue and user autonomy.

Beyond platform responsibility, addressing misinformation requires a societal commitment to digital literacy. Educating users on how to identify credible sources, understand bias, and verify information is essential for fostering a more informed public. By promoting digital literacy, individuals become empowered to discern credible information from false narratives, reducing the overall impact of misinformation on society. In an era where information is abundant but credibility is in question, fostering critical thinking is crucial for navigating social media responsibly and ensuring a well-informed, resilient society.

CHAPTER 8

The Ethical Implications of Artificial Intelligence

Artificial intelligence (AI) stands as one of the most transformative and rapidly advancing technologies of our time, with the potential to revolutionize industries, enhance productivity, and improve our daily lives in countless ways. However, alongside these remarkable benefits, the rapid development and deployment of AI raise significant ethical concerns that must be carefully considered and addressed. In this chapter, we will delve deeply into the ethical implications of AI, exploring the challenges it presents and the responsibilities of developers, policymakers, and society as a whole in navigating this complex and evolving landscape.

One of the most pressing ethical concerns surrounding AI is the issue of bias. AI systems are typically trained on large datasets, and if these datasets contain biased or unrepresentative information, the resulting AI models can perpetuate and even amplify these biases. This is particularly concerning in areas such as hiring, law enforcement, and healthcare, where biased AI algorithms can have far-reaching and potentially harmful consequences. For example, AI algorithms used in hiring processes may inadvertently discriminate against certain groups if the training data reflects historical biases in the workforce. Similarly, AI systems employed in criminal justice, such as predictive policing tools, can perpetuate racial biases if they are trained on data that reflects biased policing practices. These biases can lead to unfair treatment, perpetuation of stereotypes, and a loss of trust in AI systems, raising important questions about the fairness and accountability of AI-driven decision-making.

Addressing bias in AI requires a multifaceted approach that involves the entire AI development lifecycle. Developers must be vigilant in identifying and mitigating biases in the data and algorithms they create, using diverse and representative datasets, regularly auditing AI systems for bias, and implementing fairness measures to ensure that AI decisions are equitable. Policymakers also have a critical role to play in setting standards and regulations that promote transparency, accountability, and fairness in AI development and deployment. This may include requiring companies to conduct bias audits, mandating the use of explainable AI techniques, and ensuring that AI systems are subject to independent oversight.

Additionally, fostering a culture of ethical AI development, where developers are encouraged to consider the broader social implications of their work, is essential to creating AI systems that are both innovative and just.

Another ethical challenge posed by AI is the potential for job displacement. As AI systems become increasingly capable of performing tasks that were once the exclusive domain of humans, there is growing concern that many jobs could become obsolete. This is particularly true in industries such as manufacturing, where automation has already replaced many manual jobs. However, AI is also making inroads into white-collar professions, such as finance, legal services, and healthcare, raising concerns about the future of work in these sectors. The displacement of jobs by AI could lead to significant economic disruption, with potentially devastating effects on workers and communities. The fear of widespread job loss due to AI and automation has sparked debates about the need for retraining programs, social safety nets, and new economic models to support workers in transition.

While AI has the potential to displace jobs, it also creates new opportunities for innovation, growth, and the emergence of entirely new industries. The challenge lies in ensuring that the benefits of AI are shared equitably across society and that workers are supported in transitioning to new roles and industries. This may involve investing in education and training programs that help workers develop the skills needed to thrive in an AI-driven economy. Governments and businesses must work together to create social safety nets, such as unemployment benefits and retraining programs, to protect workers from the negative impacts of technological change. Additionally, there is a need for policies that promote job creation in sectors that are less susceptible to automation, such as creative industries, care work, and renewable energy. By proactively addressing the potential for job displacement, society can harness the benefits of AI while minimizing its disruptive effects.

Privacy is another significant ethical concern related to AI, particularly as AI systems often rely on vast amounts of data to function effectively. This data can include sensitive personal information, raising questions about how it is collected, stored, and used. The widespread use of AI in areas such as surveillance, targeted advertising, and healthcare amplifies these concerns, as there is a risk that AI systems could infringe on individuals' privacy, either through unauthorized data collection or by making decisions that affect people's lives without their knowledge or consent. The potential for AI to be used in ways that violate privacy rights underscores the need for robust data protection measures and transparent AI practices.

Ensuring that AI systems respect privacy requires a commitment to transparency, data minimization, and user control. This includes giving individuals greater control over their data, such as the ability to opt out of data collection, request the deletion of their data, and understand how their data is being used by AI systems. Developers should adopt privacy-by-design principles, incorporating privacy protections into the development of AI systems from the outset. Techniques such as differential privacy, encryption, and anonymization can help protect sensitive information while still enabling AI systems to function effectively. Policymakers should also establish clear regulations that govern the use of AI in ways that protect privacy and ensure that individuals have recourse in cases where their privacy rights are violated. By prioritizing privacy in AI development, society can build trust in AI technologies and ensure that they are used in ways that respect individual rights and freedoms.

The use of AI in decision-making processes also raises ethical questions about accountability and transparency. AI systems are increasingly being used to make decisions in areas such as credit scoring, hiring, and criminal justice, where the consequences of these decisions can have a significant impact on individuals' lives. However, the complexity of AI algorithms and the opacity of their decision-making processes can make it difficult to understand how these decisions are made, leading to concerns about transparency and accountability. This "black box" nature of AI systems can undermine trust in AI and exacerbate concerns about bias and fairness.

To address these concerns, it is essential to ensure that AI systems are transparent, explainable, and subject to accountability mechanisms. This means that AI decisions should be understandable to humans, and there should be mechanisms in place to hold AI systems accountable for their decisions. Developers should prioritize the use of explainable AI techniques that allow users to understand how and why AI systems make certain decisions. Additionally, legal and regulatory frameworks should be established to ensure that individuals have the right to challenge AI decisions that affect them and to seek redress if they believe they have been treated unfairly. By enhancing transparency and accountability in AI decision-making, society can build trust in AI systems and ensure that they are used in ways that are fair, just, and ethical.

Finally, the ethical implications of AI extend to the broader societal impact of AI technologies. As AI systems become more integrated into our daily lives, there is a risk that they could exacerbate existing inequalities or create new forms of discrimination. For example, AI-driven economic growth could disproportionately benefit certain regions, industries, or demographic groups, leaving others behind. Similarly, the deployment of AI in areas such as law enforcement, immigration control, or social services could lead to the disproportionate targeting of certain groups or the reinforcement of existing biases. These broader societal impacts raise important ethical questions about fairness, equity, and the long-term consequences of AI adoption.

Addressing these broader societal impacts requires a commitment to fairness and equity in AI development and deployment. This includes ensuring that AI technologies are accessible to all, regardless of their background or circumstances, and that they do not perpetuate or exacerbate existing inequalities. Policymakers, developers, and civil society must work together to ensure that AI technologies are developed and deployed in ways that promote social justice and contribute to a more equitable society. This may involve creating incentives for the development of AI solutions that address social challenges, such as poverty, inequality, and environmental sustainability, and ensuring that the benefits of AI are shared broadly across society. By fostering a more inclusive and equitable approach to AI development, society can harness the transformative potential of AI while minimizing its risks and ensuring that it contributes to the greater good.

While AI has the potential to bring about significant benefits, it also raises important ethical challenges that must be addressed. By adopting a proactive approach to AI ethics, we can ensure that AI technologies are developed and deployed in a way that is fair, transparent, and accountable, and that they contribute to a more just and equitable society. The ethical implications of AI are not just a technical issue; they are a societal issue that requires careful consideration and thoughtful action. As we continue to advance AI technologies, it is essential that we do so with a deep commitment to ethical principles and a focus on the common good, ensuring that AI serves as a force for positive change in the world.

Bias in AI Systems: Understanding and Addressing Algorithmic Inequality

One of the most complex ethical issues surrounding artificial intelligence lies in the problem of bias. AI systems are built by training on extensive datasets, and these datasets often include inherent biases that are reflective of historical and social prejudices. If unchecked, these biases can perpetuate or even intensify disparities. This concern is especially pressing in high-stakes fields like hiring, law enforcement, and healthcare, where the consequences of biased algorithms can lead to inequitable outcomes and, in some cases, human rights violations. For instance, an AI model used in recruitment might unconsciously favor candidates from certain demographics if trained on a dataset that reflects past hiring preferences. Similarly, predictive policing algorithms trained on biased historical data have shown tendencies to disproportionately target minority communities, often leading to over-policing and reinforced stereotypes. These biases not only affect individuals but also erode trust in AI systems and decision-makers, highlighting an urgent need to prioritize fairness and accountability in AI applications.

Addressing bias in AI is a multi-layered challenge that demands intervention at every stage of AI development. At the initial stage, developers must carefully curate datasets to ensure diversity and representativeness, removing as much biased content as possible. Moreover, techniques such as fairness-aware machine learning, in which models are adjusted to address historical imbalances, are essential tools to minimize the risk of bias in decision-making. Regular auditing and transparency are equally critical, as they enable developers to identify and rectify unintentional biases that emerge in real-world applications. Beyond technical solutions, policy frameworks are needed to enforce these standards. Laws may require mandatory bias testing, transparency reports, and explainable AI methods for applications in critical areas such as healthcare and criminal justice. This legal oversight can ensure AI systems are designed and maintained ethically. By fostering collaboration among developers, policymakers, and communities, society can work toward creating AI systems that serve the broader public fairly and responsibly, emphasizing ethical AI development and mitigating the social harms of algorithmic bias.

The Potential for Job Displacement: Navigating AI's Economic Impact on the Workforce

The potential for job displacement is one of the most significant economic and ethical implications of AI. Automation and AI technologies are becoming increasingly sophisticated, able to handle complex tasks traditionally performed by human workers. In fields like manufacturing, transportation, finance, and even healthcare, AI is not only automating manual labor but is also beginning to take over tasks that require analysis, decision-making, and customer interaction. This trend has fueled concerns about widespread job displacement, where entire industries might be reshaped, and millions of workers could face redundancy. While AI's efficiency and cost-savings appeal to industries, the disruption caused by AI-driven automation could lead to economic inequality, as the gap widens between those who can benefit from new technological skills and those left behind. Additionally, as AI moves into white-collar roles, such as data processing, customer service, and financial analysis, even higher-skilled positions are at risk, sparking concerns about the long-term stability of middle-class jobs.

While AI threatens some jobs, it also has the potential to create new employment opportunities, as with past technological revolutions. The key challenge lies in ensuring that these opportunities are accessible and sustainable. Governments, corporations, and educational institutions must collaborate to develop robust retraining and upskilling programs, helping workers transition into emerging industries. For example, workers displaced from manufacturing could be retrained for roles in renewable energy, healthcare, or AI-related fields, all of which are expected to grow as society adapts to new technological realities. Moreover, policymakers must consider strengthening social safety nets, including unemployment benefits and healthcare access, to protect those facing job loss or transitioning to new careers. Some have proposed ideas like universal basic income as a buffer against potential widespread displacement. Finally, creating incentives for growth in sectors resilient to automation such as creative industries, social work, and environmental conservation could offer alternative paths for workers displaced by AI. Successfully navigating the potential impacts of job displacement will require a holistic approach that considers social, economic, and educational policies to ensure that society benefits as a whole from AI's advancements, balancing economic growth with social responsibility.

Privacy in the Age of AI: Balancing Data-Driven Innovation with Personal Rights

As AI technology increasingly permeates daily life, the need to address privacy concerns has never been more urgent. AI relies on extensive data to function effectively, often processing sensitive personal information, such as health records, online activity, or geographic locations. This raises ethical issues regarding how this data is collected, stored, and used, particularly when people may be unaware of how their information is being employed in AI-driven systems. In areas such as targeted advertising, healthcare, and surveillance, AI can present significant privacy risks by analyzing and making decisions based on personal data. The potential misuse of this data, either through unauthorized access or breaches, underscores the need for transparent, ethical, and responsible data practices. For instance, while AI-driven health diagnostics can enhance patient care, the collection of intimate health details for machine learning models raises questions about consent, data security, and individual rights.

Privacy protection in AI requires a multi-faceted approach, integrating technological solutions with robust regulatory frameworks. Techniques like data minimization, where only essential data is collected, and anonymization or encryption of data during processing can help safeguard individual privacy. Furthermore, developers can adopt privacy-by-design principles, incorporating data protection features into AI systems from their inception. Regulatory bodies play an essential role in setting standards for privacy, with frameworks like the General Data Protection Regulation (GDPR) in the European Union offering a strong example of enforcing data rights for citizens. Laws mandating user control such as the right to access, correct, or delete personal data help empower individuals to maintain oversight of their information. Innovations in privacy-preserving AI, such as differential privacy, enable data analysis without exposing individual data points, allowing systems to learn from patterns without compromising personal details. As privacy concerns evolve with AI, establishing a global culture of transparency, data sovereignty, and ethical oversight will be crucial to building public trust in AI applications and ensuring that privacy rights remain safeguarded as technology advances.

Accountability and Transparency: Navigating the "Black Box" Problem in AI

One of the most challenging ethical issues in AI is the "black box" problem, where AI systems, especially those using deep learning, make decisions in ways that are often opaque to both users and developers. This lack of transparency is particularly concerning in high-stakes applications where AI's decisions can significantly impact people's lives, such as in criminal justice, healthcare, and finance. When AI algorithms determine whether someone qualifies for a loan, is eligible for parole, or receives a particular medical treatment, the inability to fully understand or explain these decisions raises critical questions about accountability. Moreover, without transparency, it is difficult for developers to identify and address potential biases or errors within these systems. The complexity of these algorithms, combined with proprietary protections around AI models, can prevent even the developers from understanding how specific inputs lead to particular outputs. This opacity can breed mistrust in AI, particularly when individuals affected by AI decisions are unable to contest or fully comprehend the basis for these outcomes.

Enhancing accountability and transparency in AI requires concerted efforts from both technology developers and policymakers. Explainable AI (XAI) techniques are being developed to make algorithms more interpretable, allowing users to trace and understand AI's decision-making processes. For example, developers can create models that provide reasoning in a human-comprehensible format or produce visualizations that reveal which factors influence certain outcomes. Additionally, regulators can establish standards for transparency, especially in sectors where AI's decisions directly affect individual rights and welfare. Legal requirements for transparency, regular audits, and documentation of AI's decision-making processes could foster accountability, as could independent oversight bodies tasked with reviewing and evaluating AI models. Furthermore, individuals should have the right to appeal or request explanations for AI decisions that impact them, empowering them to seek justice when necessary. By prioritizing transparency and accountability, society can enhance trust in AI technologies, ensuring that AI systems operate ethically and responsibly while safeguarding the rights and welfare of individuals affected by these systems.

CHAPTER 9

The Rise of Blockchain and Decentralization

Blockchain technology has emerged as one of the most transformative and disruptive innovations of the 21st century, with the potential to revolutionize industries, reshape governance, and redefine the way we conduct transactions on a global scale. Originally developed as the underlying technology for Bitcoin, blockchain has since evolved into a versatile tool with applications far beyond cryptocurrencies. In this chapter, we will explore the rise of blockchain technology and the broader trend of decentralization, examining how these innovations are reshaping industries, governance, and society as a whole, and considering the challenges and opportunities they present.

At its core, blockchain is a distributed ledger technology that allows data to be stored across a network of computers in a secure, transparent, and immutable manner. Unlike traditional centralized databases, where data is controlled by a single entity, blockchain distributes control across a network of participants, ensuring that no single party has unilateral power over the system. This decentralization is one of the key features that sets blockchain apart from other technologies and has fueled its adoption across a wide range of industries, from finance and supply chain management to healthcare and public administration.

One of the most well-known applications of blockchain is in the realm of cryptocurrencies. Bitcoin, the first and most widely recognized cryptocurrency, introduced the concept of a decentralized digital currency that operates without the need for a central authority, such as a bank or government. Bitcoin transactions are recorded on a blockchain, providing transparency and security while enabling peer-to-peer transactions across the globe. The success of Bitcoin has led to the creation of thousands of other cryptocurrencies, each with its unique features and use cases, including Ethereum, Ripple, and Litecoin. These cryptocurrencies have sparked a global movement towards decentralized finance (DeFi), where financial transactions and services are conducted without the need for traditional intermediaries.

Beyond cryptocurrencies, blockchain technology is being applied in a wide range of industries, with the potential to transform the way we conduct business and manage information. In the financial sector, blockchain is being used to streamline processes such as cross-border payments, reducing the time and cost associated with traditional methods. For example, blockchain-based remittance services allow individuals to send money across borders quickly and at a fraction of the cost of traditional wire transfers. Blockchain technology is also being explored for its potential to improve transparency and reduce fraud in areas such as securities trading, where the immutable nature of blockchain records can provide a clear and auditable trail of transactions.

In supply chain management, blockchain is being used to track the movement of goods from production to delivery, providing greater transparency and reducing the risk of fraud. By recording every step of a product's journey on a blockchain, companies can ensure the authenticity of their products and provide consumers with greater confidence in the supply chain. This is particularly important in industries such as food and pharmaceuticals, where the ability to trace the origin and handling of products can have significant implications for safety and quality. Blockchain's ability to provide a transparent and immutable record of transactions is transforming supply chain management, creating new opportunities for efficiency and accountability.

Blockchain's potential to transform industries extends to the realm of governance and public administration. Decentralized applications (dApps) built on blockchain platforms offer the possibility of creating more transparent and accountable systems of governance. For example, blockchain-based voting systems can provide a secure and transparent way to conduct elections, reducing the risk of tampering and ensuring that votes are accurately counted. Similarly, blockchain can be used to create transparent public records, such as land registries, that are resistant to corruption and fraud. These applications demonstrate the potential of blockchain to improve transparency, reduce corruption, and enhance trust in public institutions, creating a more accountable and equitable system of governance.

Another key aspect of blockchain technology is the concept of smart contracts. Smart contracts are self-executing agreements with the terms of the contract directly written into code. These contracts automatically execute and enforce themselves when certain conditions are met, without the need for intermediaries. Smart contracts have the potential to revolutionize industries such as real estate, law, and insurance, where contracts are a fundamental part of business transactions. For example, in real estate, a smart contract could automatically transfer ownership of a property once payment is received, streamlining the process and reducing the need for legal intermediaries. In insurance, smart contracts could automate the claims process, reducing the time and cost associated with manual claims processing and improving the overall efficiency of the industry.

The broader trend of decentralization, which blockchain is a part of, is also reshaping the way organizations and communities operate. Decentralized Autonomous Organizations (DAOs) are a new form of organization that operates on a blockchain, with decision-making processes governed by smart contracts and the collective voting of participants. DAOs represent a shift away from traditional hierarchical structures, offering a more democratic and transparent way to manage organizations. This has the potential to transform industries such as finance, where DAOs can be used to manage investment funds or other financial products in a decentralized manner. The rise of DAOs is part of a broader movement towards decentralization, where power and control are distributed among participants rather than concentrated in the hands of a few, creating new opportunities for innovation and collaboration.

However, the rise of blockchain and decentralization is not without challenges. One of the most significant challenges is the issue of scalability. As blockchain networks grow, the amount of data that needs to be processed and stored increases, leading to potential bottlenecks and slower transaction times. This is particularly true for public blockchains, where every participant must validate transactions. Solutions such as layer 2 scaling, sharding, and improved consensus algorithms are being developed to address these issues, but scalability remains a critical challenge for widespread adoption. Ensuring that blockchain networks can scale effectively while maintaining security and decentralization is essential to realizing the full potential of the technology.

Another challenge is the regulatory environment. The decentralized nature of blockchain and cryptocurrencies poses a challenge for regulators, who must balance the need to protect consumers and prevent illegal activities with the desire to foster innovation. Different countries have taken varying approaches to regulating blockchain and cryptocurrencies, with some embracing the technology and others imposing strict regulations. The lack of a consistent global regulatory framework creates uncertainty for businesses and investors, potentially hindering the growth of the blockchain ecosystem. Developing clear and consistent regulations that promote innovation while protecting consumers is essential to the long-term success of blockchain technology.

Security is also a major concern in the world of blockchain. While blockchain technology is inherently secure due to its decentralized nature and cryptographic techniques, it is not immune to attacks. Hacks and exploits, particularly on decentralized finance (DeFi) platforms, have resulted in significant financial losses and undermined trust in the technology. Ensuring the security of blockchain networks and applications is an ongoing challenge that requires continuous innovation and vigilance. This includes addressing vulnerabilities in smart contracts, securing private keys, and implementing robust security measures to protect against attacks. By prioritizing security, the blockchain community can build trust in the technology and ensure its long-term success.

Despite these challenges, the potential of blockchain and decentralization to transform industries and society is immense. By enabling greater transparency, security, and efficiency, blockchain has the potential to disrupt traditional systems and create new opportunities for innovation and growth. As the technology continues to evolve, it will be essential to address the challenges and ensure that blockchain is used in a way that benefits society as a whole. This may involve developing new governance models, establishing best practices for security and scalability, and creating regulatory frameworks that balance innovation with consumer protection.

This technology and the broader trend of decentralization represent a paradigm shift in how we think about data, transactions, and governance. While there are significant challenges to overcome, the potential benefits of blockchain are vast, offering new opportunities for transparency, security, and efficiency across a wide range of industries. As we continue to explore the possibilities of blockchain and decentralization, it is essential to ensure that these technologies are developed and deployed in a way that promotes equity, transparency, and trust. By doing so, we can harness the power of blockchain to create a more just, inclusive, and resilient society, paving the way for a future where technology serves the common good.

Blockchain: The Foundation of a New Digital Era

Blockchain technology has introduced an entirely new paradigm in the way data, transactions, and trust are managed in the digital world. At its core, blockchain functions as a decentralized ledger, one where every participant in the network has access to an identical record of transactions, and every block added to the chain is immutable and transparent. This fundamental architecture has paved the way for a novel approach to digital trust, as it allows information to be verified without a central authority. Unlike traditional centralized systems where trust is often consolidated in one institution, blockchain redistributes control across a network of independent nodes, which democratizes data ownership and increases security. This redistribution of control forms the bedrock of blockchain's influence, especially as more people and organizations look to create systems that are transparent and resistant to tampering.

In addition to its decentralized nature, blockchain operates on principles that allow data to be stored in a chronological, cryptographically secured, and public manner. Each block, once created, is interlinked with previous blocks using a unique cryptographic hash, making it almost impossible to alter or remove information without the consensus of the network. This level of security is a game-changer for industries that rely on data integrity and authenticity, such as finance, healthcare, and supply chain management. Blockchain's commitment to transparency and traceability has the potential to reshape how trust is built in digital transactions, and its applications are expanding at a rapid pace as more industries adopt it as a foundation for secure, verifiable records.

Moreover, as a technology with decentralized properties, blockchain serves as a launching point for a broader movement toward "Web 3.0" the concept of a decentralized web. While Web 2.0 enabled user-generated content and interactivity, Web 3.0 seeks to remove reliance on large, centralized platforms, bringing users closer to full control over their digital identities and data. Blockchain, in this context, is seen as the infrastructure on which users can own, monetize, and securely manage their data. This foundational shift marks an evolution from merely consuming or sharing content to truly owning and controlling digital assets and information. As blockchain adoption continues, it will be integral to creating systems that prioritize user autonomy and data sovereignty, making it a pivotal technology in building the new digital era.

Cryptocurrencies and the Decentralized Finance Revolution

Cryptocurrencies represent one of the most widely recognized applications of blockchain technology, but their influence goes beyond just providing a digital alternative to traditional currencies. Cryptocurrencies like Bitcoin, Ethereum, and thousands of others have spawned an entirely new financial ecosystem known as decentralized finance (DeFi). Unlike traditional financial institutions that act as intermediaries for banking services, DeFi leverages blockchain's decentralized nature to allow users to engage in financial activities such as lending, borrowing, trading, and investing without the need for banks or other intermediaries. By doing so, DeFi aims to democratize access to financial services, offering a solution to the billions of people worldwide who remain unbanked or underserved by traditional finance systems.

In the decentralized finance ecosystem, smart contracts enable users to interact directly with each other and the blockchain network, creating peer-to-peer financial networks that operate transparently. For example, DeFi platforms often use lending pools, where participants can deposit assets to earn interest or borrow against them, with all conditions and rates governed by smart contracts. This system removes the need for a third party to mediate or administer transactions, creating a financial environment that operates 24/7 and is accessible to anyone with an internet connection. Additionally, the transparency provided by blockchain means that users can verify the integrity of these systems, as all transactions are publicly recorded and can be audited in real-time.

The rise of DeFi also introduces new financial instruments, including stablecoins, liquidity pools, and decentralized exchanges, that were previously unavailable to the average person. Stablecoins, for example, offer a bridge between volatile cryptocurrencies and traditional currencies by pegging their value to a stable asset like the U.S. dollar. These developments offer more versatility, as individuals can interact with a global financial system that doesn't fluctuate wildly, ensuring a more stable environment for savings and transactions. As DeFi continues to grow, it's transforming finance into a decentralized, accessible, and borderless system that empowers users with financial freedom and flexibility while challenging traditional banking institutions to innovate and adapt to a new financial paradigm.

Blockchain Beyond Finance: Transforming Industries Globally

While finance has been an early and prominent adopter of blockchain, this technology has the potential to fundamentally transform numerous other industries as well. The decentralized and transparent nature of blockchain is particularly well-suited to sectors that require robust data verification, traceability, and security. In supply chain management, for instance, blockchain allows every stage of a product's journey from raw materials to final delivery to be tracked and documented in an immutable ledger. This means that consumers can have confidence in the authenticity and quality of the products they purchase, and companies can quickly identify and address issues in the supply chain, whether it be counterfeit goods, contamination, or other risks.

The healthcare industry, too, is exploring blockchain for its ability to enhance data security, privacy, and interoperability. Patient data, medical histories, and treatment records can be securely stored and shared on blockchain networks, allowing healthcare providers to access comprehensive and accurate patient information while protecting sensitive data. Moreover, blockchain's decentralized structure could enable the creation of personal health records controlled by the patients themselves, allowing individuals to share their health data with providers on a need-to-know basis. This shift not only empowers patients with greater control over their personal information but also has the potential to reduce medical errors, streamline administrative processes, and improve patient outcomes.

Another significant area of impact is intellectual property (IP) and digital rights management. Blockchain provides a way to establish proof of ownership for digital assets, making it possible for creators, such as artists, musicians, and writers, to protect and monetize their work in a way that is secure and verifiable. Through non-fungible tokens (NFTs), blockchain offers creators a method to register ownership of unique digital assets, which can be bought, sold, and traded on the blockchain. This development is reshaping the creative industries, providing a new revenue stream for artists while combating issues such as copyright infringement and unauthorized duplication. The use of blockchain in IP protection highlights its versatility and potential to impact a wide range of industries beyond finance.

Smart Contracts and the Automation of Trust

Smart contracts are one of the most innovative aspects of blockchain technology, representing a shift in how agreements are formed, executed, and enforced. Unlike traditional contracts, which require legal intermediaries to ensure compliance, smart contracts are self-executing agreements written directly into code that automatically enforce the terms and conditions agreed upon by the parties involved. Once the predefined conditions of a smart contract are met, the contract executes itself, eliminating the need for middlemen and reducing the costs, time, and potential errors associated with manual contract enforcement. This automation of trust allows individuals and businesses to conduct transactions with confidence, as they can rely on the integrity of the code rather than the reliability of a third party.

Smart contracts have applications across various industries, enabling the automation of processes in ways that streamline operations and reduce the need for intermediaries. In real estate, for instance, smart contracts can simplify property transactions by automating tasks like verifying ownership, transferring funds, and recording deeds on the blockchain. This reduces the complexity of real estate deals, cutting down on paperwork, fees, and processing times. In insurance, smart contracts allow for faster and more accurate claims processing. For example, a travel insurance policy executed through a smart contract could automatically issue a payout if a flight is delayed or canceled, as the contract could verify the flight's status through external data sources and trigger a payout without requiring the policyholder to file a claim manually.

Beyond these practical applications, smart contracts are central to the growth of decentralized applications (dApps) and decentralized autonomous organizations (DAOs). These entities operate through smart contracts, enabling communities to self-govern and make decisions collectively without the need for a traditional management hierarchy. In DAOs, voting processes, project funding, and operational rules are managed by smart contracts, ensuring transparency and accountability. This decentralized model empowers members with an equitable stake in the organization's decisions, providing a glimpse into a new way of coordinating human activity based on shared goals and values. Smart contracts are not merely technical tools; they are at the heart of the ongoing transformation toward decentralized systems, fundamentally changing how trust and agreements are managed in a digital world.

NURUDEEN D. NURUDEEN

CHAPTER 10
The Global Digital Divide

As technology continues to advance at an unprecedented pace, transforming economies, societies, and individual lives around the world, it is becoming increasingly clear that the benefits of this digital revolution are not being experienced equally by all. The global digital divide refers to the gap between those who have access to modern information and communication technologies (ICTs) and those who do not, creating disparities in opportunities, resources, and outcomes. This divide exists both between and within countries, and it has significant implications for economic development, education, healthcare, and social inclusion. In this chapter, we will explore the causes, consequences, and potential solutions to the global digital divide, with a focus on how to bridge this gap and ensure that the benefits of technology are shared equitably across all segments of society.

The digital divide can be attributed to a variety of factors, including economic disparities, geographic location, and infrastructure development. In many low-income countries, the cost of acquiring and maintaining digital devices such as smartphones, computers, and tablets is prohibitively high for large segments of the population. Additionally, access to reliable and affordable internet services remains limited in many rural and remote areas, where the necessary infrastructure is often lacking. This lack of access to digital technologies exacerbates existing inequalities and limits opportunities for individuals and communities to participate in the digital economy. For example, individuals without access to digital technologies may struggle to find employment, access education, or obtain essential services, further entrenching cycles of poverty and exclusion.

Education is one of the areas most affected by the digital divide, with significant implications for students, educators, and societies as a whole. In today's world, digital literacy is increasingly essential for accessing educational resources, participating in online learning, and acquiring the skills needed for the modern workforce. However, in regions where access to digital technologies is limited, students and educators face significant barriers to effective learning. The COVID-19 pandemic highlighted these disparities, as schools around the world shifted to online learning, leaving many students in low-income and rural areas without the tools they needed to continue their education. This has resulted in a widening gap in educational attainment between those with access to digital technologies and those without, raising concerns about the long-term impact on social mobility and economic opportunity.

The digital divide also has significant implications for healthcare, particularly in underserved and remote areas where access to healthcare services is already limited. Telemedicine and digital health tools have the potential to improve access to healthcare services, enabling remote consultations, monitoring, and treatment. However, the lack of digital infrastructure and access to technology in these areas means that many people are unable to benefit from these advancements. This exacerbates existing health disparities and limits the ability of healthcare providers to reach those most in need. Additionally, the lack of digital literacy can prevent individuals from effectively using digital health tools, further limiting their ability to access care and manage their health.

Economic opportunities are another area where the digital divide has a profound impact, creating disparities in income, employment, and entrepreneurship. The digital economy offers numerous opportunities for entrepreneurship, job creation, and economic growth, with digital platforms enabling businesses to reach new markets, streamline operations, and innovate. However, individuals and communities without access to digital technologies are often excluded from these opportunities, limiting their ability to participate fully in the economy and improve their economic prospects. This can result in a cycle of poverty and marginalization, as those without access to technology are unable to take advantage of the opportunities offered by the digital economy. The digital divide also affects businesses, particularly small and medium-sized enterprises (SMEs), which may struggle to compete in a globalized market without access to digital tools and resources.

Addressing the global digital divide requires a multifaceted approach that involves governments, the private sector, and civil society working together to expand access to digital technologies and bridge the gap between those with and without access. Investment in digital infrastructure is essential to expanding access to technology in underserved areas, including the expansion of broadband networks, the deployment of affordable devices, and the provision of digital literacy training. Public-private partnerships can play a key role in driving these efforts, with companies providing the necessary technology and expertise while governments create the enabling environment through policies and regulations that promote digital inclusion and accessibility.

In addition to infrastructure development, it is important to address the affordability of digital technologies, as high costs can be a significant barrier to access for low-income individuals and communities. Subsidies and financing programs can help make devices and internet services more affordable, enabling more people to access the benefits of the digital economy. Innovative business models, such as community-owned networks and low-cost internet service providers, can also help bridge the affordability gap by offering affordable and sustainable solutions tailored to the needs of underserved communities. Governments can also play a role by implementing policies that promote competition in the telecommunications sector, driving down prices and increasing access to affordable services for all.

Education and digital literacy are critical components of efforts to bridge the digital divide, as they provide individuals with the skills and knowledge needed to navigate the digital world and take advantage of the opportunities it offers. Governments and educational institutions must prioritize digital literacy training, ensuring that individuals have the skills they need to succeed in the digital age. This includes not only basic computer skills but also more advanced skills such as coding, data analysis, and digital content creation, which are increasingly in demand in the modern workforce. Providing access to digital learning resources, both online and offline, is also essential to ensuring that all students have the opportunity to succeed in the digital age. Additionally, initiatives that promote lifelong learning and continuous skill development can help individuals adapt to the changing demands of the digital economy and stay competitive in a rapidly evolving job market.

Finally, addressing the digital divide requires a focus on inclusivity, ensuring that efforts to bridge the divide are designed to meet the needs of marginalized and vulnerable populations, including women, people with disabilities, and indigenous communities. This includes designing digital technologies and services that are accessible to all, as well as ensuring that these groups are represented in decision-making processes related to digital development. For example, promoting gender equity in the technology sector and supporting initiatives that empower women and girls to pursue careers in STEM (science, technology, engineering, and mathematics) can help reduce gender disparities in access to digital technologies and create a more inclusive digital economy. Additionally, efforts to promote digital inclusion should take into account the unique needs and challenges faced by different communities, ensuring that solutions are tailored to local contexts and priorities.

The global digital divide is a significant challenge that must be addressed to ensure that the benefits of the digital revolution are shared equitably across all segments of society. By investing in digital infrastructure, improving affordability, prioritizing digital literacy, and promoting inclusivity, we can bridge the divide and create a more connected, inclusive, and prosperous world. The digital divide is not just a technological issue; it is a social and economic issue that requires a coordinated and sustained effort to address. As we move forward, it is essential that we work together to ensure that no one is left behind in the digital age, and that the opportunities and benefits of technology are accessible to all, regardless of their background or circumstances.

Infrastructure Gaps: The Foundation of Digital Disparities

The digital divide is deeply rooted in the foundational infrastructure required for internet connectivity, including reliable power sources, telecommunication towers, and network cables. Many countries in low-income and developing regions lack the necessary resources to build and maintain such infrastructure, particularly in remote and rural areas. For these communities, the absence of adequate infrastructure means limited or nonexistent internet connectivity, leaving entire populations unable to participate in the digital revolution. In developed regions, on the other hand, internet access is often treated as an essential utility, much like water and electricity, with extensive coverage reaching even sparsely populated areas.

However, in countries with limited resources or challenging terrains, installing and maintaining physical infrastructure can be prohibitively expensive. In places like Sub-Saharan Africa and parts of Southeast Asia, these financial and logistical barriers create a stark divide between urban centers where connectivity may be relatively accessible and rural areas that remain largely disconnected. Moreover, unreliable power sources in certain regions hinder consistent internet access even where basic network infrastructure exists, creating an additional obstacle to connectivity.

Addressing infrastructure gaps requires a coordinated global effort, with both public and private sectors playing pivotal roles. Investment in alternative technologies like satellite internet, which can bypass traditional infrastructure needs, has shown promise in providing connectivity to remote and underserved areas. Similarly, the deployment of mobile broadband networks has helped address connectivity challenges in countries with limited infrastructure for wired internet. Some governments have partnered with technology companies to promote initiatives such as internet-for-all campaigns, building localized infrastructure that benefits entire communities. These efforts, however, are still in the early stages, and closing the infrastructure gap remains one of the most significant challenges in bridging the global digital divide. By focusing on foundational infrastructure, we can empower more individuals and communities to access digital resources and participate in the global digital economy.

The Language and Content Divide: Addressing Barriers to Digital Inclusion

Another less obvious but equally important aspect of the digital divide is the language and content gap. Despite the vast amount of information available on the internet, the majority of content is in English, followed by a handful of other dominant languages. For individuals who speak minority languages or languages that lack significant digital representation, this linguistic divide creates a barrier to meaningful internet access. Even in regions where internet access is available, limited content in the local language can reduce the utility of that access, affecting educational, economic, and social engagement opportunities.

The language divide is particularly pronounced in multilingual countries with limited representation online. For instance, while a large portion of web content is available in languages like English, Spanish, and Mandarin, indigenous languages, as well as regional dialects, are often underrepresented. This disparity can prevent people from accessing essential information, participating in online learning, and using digital tools for their personal and professional growth. As more global content is developed without consideration for language inclusivity, speakers of minority languages are often left with minimal resources and limited participation in the digital world.

To bridge the language and content divide, both governments and technology companies need to prioritize localized content and invest in language translation tools. Machine learning advancements, particularly in natural language processing (NLP), have opened doors for real-time translation and more accessible content creation. Tech companies are beginning to invest in multi-language support, translating websites and online resources into various languages, which is especially critical for regions with low literacy rates and limited internet content in native languages. Additionally, community-driven translation initiatives can empower native speakers to contribute their knowledge to digital spaces, enriching the web with more diverse perspectives. By increasing the representation of minority languages online, we can create a more inclusive internet that serves users from all linguistic backgrounds.

The Role of Digital Skills in Empowering Communities

While physical access to the internet is essential, the ability to use digital tools effectively known as digital literacy is equally important in bridging the digital divide. Digital literacy encompasses a range of skills, from basic internet navigation to more advanced competencies like coding, data analysis, and cybersecurity. Without these skills, individuals may struggle to engage meaningfully with digital platforms or fully participate in the modern workforce. Limited digital literacy can leave people vulnerable to misinformation, unable to benefit from digital resources, and at a disadvantage in the job market, particularly as economies increasingly rely on digital skills.

In many low-income regions, digital literacy rates are low, partly due to a lack of exposure to technology and limited educational resources. Schools in rural or underserved communities may lack computers, internet access, and trained educators who can teach digital skills, creating a cycle of exclusion that can last for generations. Additionally, older adults, who may not have had the opportunity to engage with technology in their youth, face unique challenges in adapting to digital environments. These skills gap not only prevents people from accessing the benefits of the digital world but also creates barriers to employment, education, and social engagement.

Addressing the digital skills gap requires investment in education and training programs, with a focus on inclusivity and accessibility. Governments and educational institutions must prioritize digital literacy in their curricula, ensuring that students are equipped with the skills they need for the digital economy. This includes partnerships between schools, non-profits, and tech companies to provide resources, training, and digital tools for underserved populations. Digital literacy programs targeting older adults, women, and marginalized communities can also help empower these groups to engage more fully with technology. By equipping individuals with digital skills, we can create a more equitable society where everyone has the opportunity to participate in the digital economy and leverage technology for personal growth.

Social and Economic Exclusion: The Broader Implications of the Digital Divide

The digital divide has far-reaching social and economic consequences that extend beyond mere access to technology. For those on the wrong side of the divide, lack of connectivity means exclusion from economic opportunities, limited access to essential services, and isolation from global and local communities. Digital technology has become a vital driver of social mobility, enabling people to access educational resources, job markets, and healthcare services that were previously out of reach. However, those without digital access are often left behind, unable to take advantage of these opportunities and facing greater risks of economic and social marginalization.

In education, for example, the digital divide limits students' ability to learn from online resources, participate in remote learning, and acquire digital skills critical for future employment. The COVID-19 pandemic has exacerbated these disparities, as students in underserved communities often lacked the devices and internet connectivity needed for online learning. This disparity in educational access can have lasting impacts on students' academic and career prospects, perpetuating cycles of poverty and limiting upward mobility.

In the realm of healthcare, the digital divide restricts access to telemedicine services, which can be particularly beneficial in remote or underserved areas where healthcare facilities are limited. For individuals in these areas, lack of access to telemedicine means that routine health check-ups, prescription renewals, and specialist consultations are challenging to obtain. Additionally, economic opportunities within the digital economy, such as remote work, e-commerce, and online freelancing, are largely inaccessible to those without internet access, leaving communities isolated from the opportunities of the modern world.

Closing the digital divide requires not only improving connectivity but also addressing the socio-economic factors that contribute to digital exclusion. Governments, non-profits, and businesses must work collaboratively to promote digital inclusion by expanding access to affordable devices and internet services, creating community centers with free internet access, and providing job training programs that equip people with the skills needed for the digital economy. Additionally, policies that support economic growth and job creation in low-income communities can help reduce digital exclusion by providing individuals with the means to access and utilize digital tools. By addressing the broader social and economic impacts of the digital divide, we can create a more inclusive society where everyone has the opportunity to thrive in the digital age.

ABOUT THE AUTHOR

Nurudeen D. Nurudeen is a distinguished software engineer and thought leader with more than eight years of hands-on experience at the intersection of technology and society. Known for his forward-thinking approach and innovative mind, Nurudeen has earned a reputation as a trailblazer within the tech community. His contributions to software engineering and his dedication to social impact earned him the prestigious Software Innovation Excellence Award from the Tech Trailblazers Visionary Prize, a recognition given only to those who push the boundaries of technological advancement with creativity and a deep sense of responsibility.

Throughout his career, Nurudeen has been driven by a single, unifying vision: to create technology that not only solves problems but also enriches lives and promotes inclusivity. His diverse portfolio includes pioneering projects in areas ranging from financial technology to AI-powered social solutions, each underscoring his commitment to ethical innovation. With a rare blend of technical prowess and strategic insight, Nurudeen consistently advocates for a future where technology aligns with humanity's most pressing needs.

In "Beyond Fintech: The Broader Impact of Technology on Society," Nurudeen combines his vast technical knowledge with a nuanced understanding of societal trends, shedding light on the far-reaching effects of technology on diverse sectors. His writing reveals not just the 'how' but the 'why' of technological impact, posing critical questions and exploring the ethical dimensions of an increasingly digital world. Whether he's discussing blockchain, smart cities, or AI, Nurudeen's approach is grounded in a commitment to making technology work for everyone. His work continues to inspire fellow technologists, business leaders, and anyone interested in harnessing the power of technology for positive, inclusive change.